BALANCED BOWHUNTING

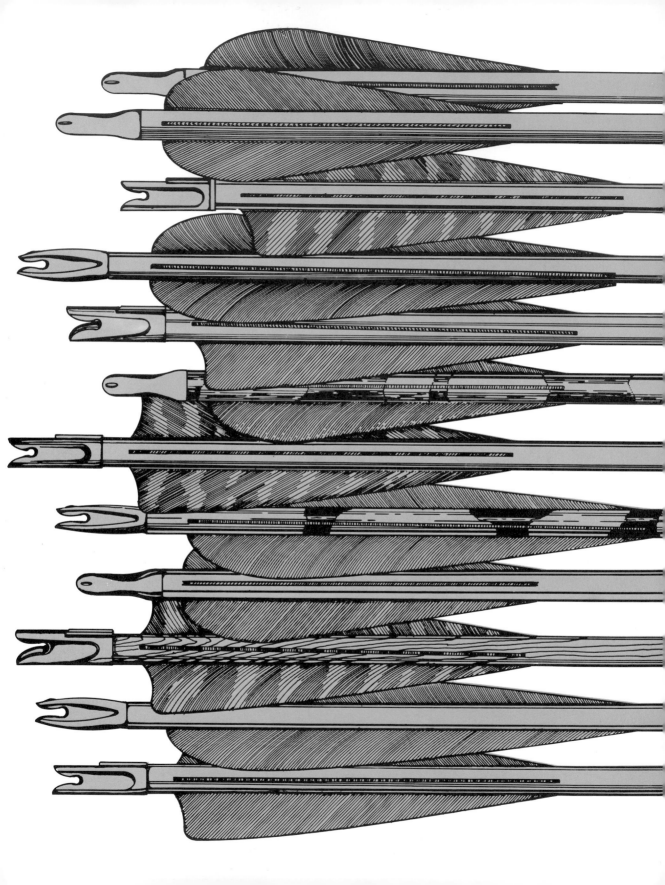

B A L A N C E D
BOWHUNTING

Dave Holt

A Guide to Modern Bowhunting

High Country Publishers
Lakewood, Colorado

Published in the United States of America by:

High Country Publishers

BALANCED BOWHUNTING

A Guide to Modern Bowhunting

Cover art by Johnnie Lujan
Text art by Monte Swan and Bill Border
Text photos by Lee Kline and the author
Wildlife photos pp. 14, 26, 38, 50, 62, 78, 90, 108, 134 and 148 by Lee Kline
Photo p. 122 by Monte Swan
Cover design by Rick Hanson
Library of Congress Catalog Number: 88-081804
ISBN 0-9620713-0-7

DEDICATION

It may seem unusual but I can backpack in the most majestic country Colorado has to offer and if I don't sense the presence of wild creatures, both large and small, that scenic beauty is diminished. Conversely, the sighting of a ringneck pheasant or whitetail deer in a stark Nebraska cornfield can leave an indelible print of beauty in my memory — a beauty that is somehow transferred to the land that nurtured them. Appropriately, this book is dedicated to America's wildlife, for it is they who have truly brought me so much joy.

ACKNOWLEDGEMENTS

Until you write a book yourself, or worse yet, help someone else write one, you probably won't have much appreciation for this page in any book. That was true in my case, until now. Without the help of the talented and creative people who so generously donated their time, this book would never have been more than some indiscernible chicken scratching on several yellow legal pads. A very special thanks goes to Chris Ruys, Monte Swan, Chuck Lane, Lee Kline, Johnnie Lujan and Dick Miller! I also want to thank the following people, all of whom helped make this book a reality.

Marie Ruys	Steve Cyphers
Mike Gordan	Jay Elmer
Norb Mullaney	Vera Wells
Larry Luterman	Dennis Wehling
M. R. James	Sheri Fraker
G. Fred Asbell	Jan & Doy Curtis
Dwight Schuh	Glen Helgeland
Jeannie & George Straw	Jerry Baines
Dan Predovich	Rob Forth
Gene Swanson	Mike Bingham
Fred Ramey	Ron & John Phillips

TABLE OF CONTENTS

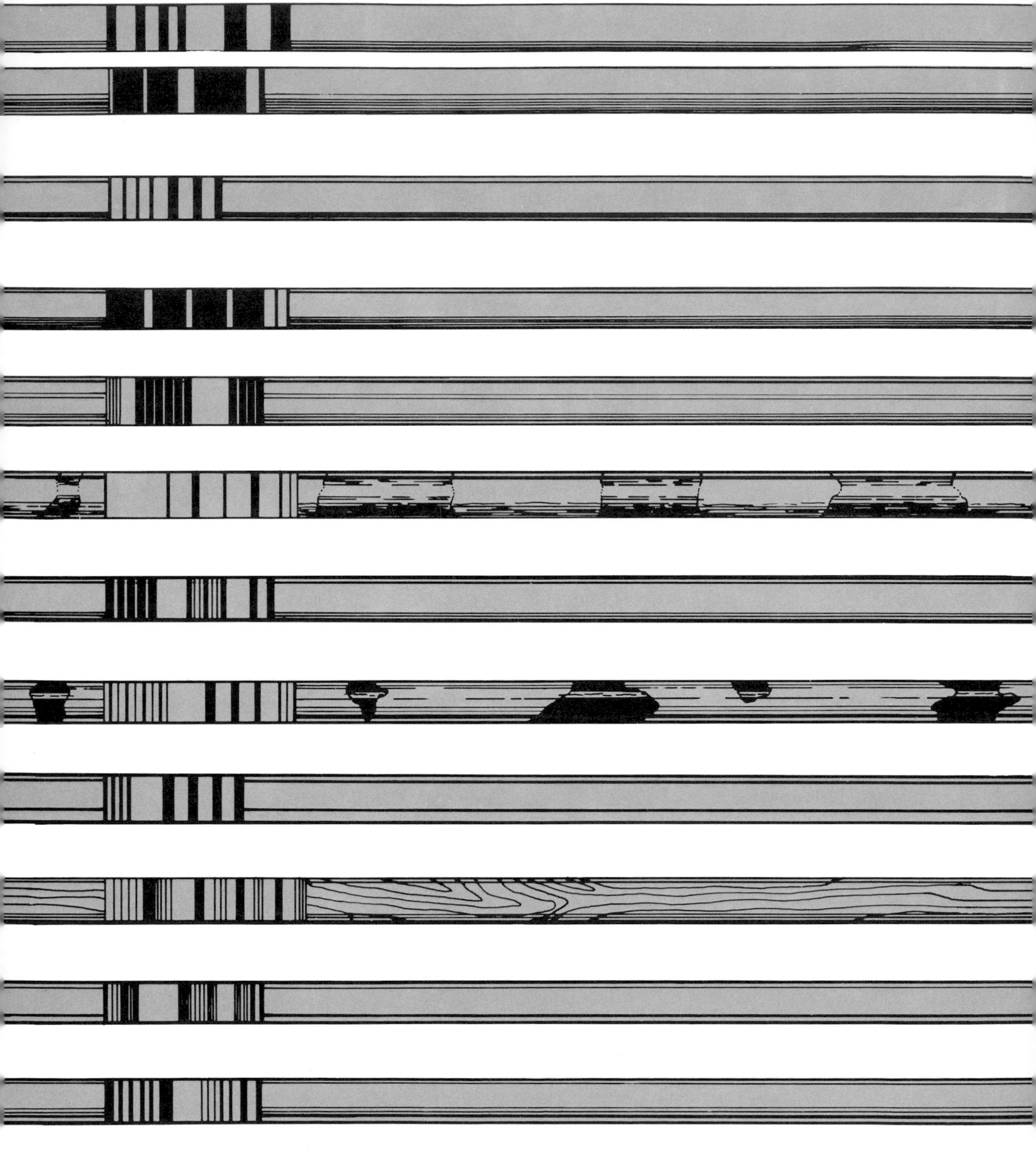

FOREWORD

Archery has changed so drastically in recent years, many of us can't keep up. New bow materials and designs, overdraws, lighter arrows, better rests, rangefinding devices, new broadhead designs, and an infinite variety of accessories and gadgets for every possible need nearly boggle our minds. These have all led to new philosophies on proper shooting distance, revised thoughts on bow efficiency, new shooting methods and changes in hunting technique.

Unfortunately, every bowhunter and writer seems to have a pet topic that promises to be a magic carpet to bowhunting success. That would be great if it worked; it would simplify things for us all. The only problem is that bowhunting is not a one-dimensional sport and no one aspect holds solutions to all the problems. Even today, with all the advanced technology in archery, a bowhunter, to succeed with any regularity, must develop a broad knowledge and a variety of skills.

And that's the thrust of Dave Holt's approach to bowhunting. As the name of his book implies, he believes in balance. Holt doesn't get carried away beating the drum for any one pet theory, system or technique. Rather, he explores all the significant aspects of modern archery and then molds them together to shape a complete bowhunting system.

One thing I like about Dave Holt's book is that it covers technicalities without being technical. Let's face it, modern archery gear is technical, and a modern bowhunter must understand the technicalities to get the most from his gear. At the same time, few of us bowhunters are technicians by nature. We're hunters who want to learn the mechanics of modern bows to hunt more efficiently. Dave Holt does a good job of explaining the technical in terms easy enough for all bowhunters to understand.

In particular, his guidelines on choosing a bow make sense. He doesn't base his advice on a conjecture that certain bows are more "sensitive" or that you must shoot a specific draw weight to kill certain animals. Rather he relies on years of experience shooting many different kinds of tackle as well as sound mathematics. Many aspects of bow selection and evaluation leave little room for dispute. Judging a bow's efficiency, for example, is a matter of mathematics, not subjective opinion. Dave Holt uses basic, indisputable formulas to demonstrate his claims.

The real danger in any book on tackle and fundamentals is reader boredom. Who wants to read a textbook of facts and figures? Most of us want to read hunting stories—something we can relate to, something that revs our motors. Dave has pulled in plenty of hunting stories from his own experience and that of his friends to keep the book flowing, to keep our interest while teaching us to be better archers and bowhunters.

For every serious modern bowhunter, I recommend Dave Holt's *Balanced Bowhunting*.

Dwight Schuh
Nampa, Idaho

INTRODUCTION

Choosing a name for this book was an incredibly difficult task, in part because the text covers two different aspects of bowhunting: the causes and cures of missing and the pros and cons of equipment. There is, however, a common message of balance throughout the book. Balance, to me, means improving all your abilities equally to the highest possible level. When dealing with equipment, it means thoroughly understanding what each item has to offer and then choosing what works best for your style of bowhunting. To accomplish these goals, you must know how to get the most from yourself and your equipment. You also need enough information and knowledge to make logical decisions about what is best for you. It is my sincere desire that the knowledge gained from this book will enable you to make your bowhunting more enjoyable, satisfying and successful.

Statistics on bowhunter success indicate the animal has the advantage, but you can certainly improve your chances for success. The information and ideas discussed in the following chapters will give you the tools to identify and strengthen your weakest skills. The goal of this book is to increase your knowledge of bowhunting equipment and improve all aspects of accurate shooting under actual hunting conditions. That balance is what ultimately produces consistent success in harvesting big game animals. Improving your skills takes a combination of desire, knowledge and experience. The best reason for putting forth the necessary effort to improve is to prepare yourself better to *humanely* harvest the game animals you intend to hunt.

When I began my bowhunting career in 1958, most knowledge had to be gained through trial and error. Fortunately for today's bowhunters, that has all changed. In recent years, there has been an enormous amount of written material aimed at increasing our knowledge on how to hunt North American big game animals of every description. There are excellent "How To Hunt..." books on bugling elk, calling turkeys, hunting whitetail and mule deer, baiting bears, etc. Most of these books are well worth reading and will go a long way toward helping you get that shot of a lifetime. But the area where information is still terribly lacking is how to become a more accurate *game shot*.

The first half of this book picks up where the "how-to-hunt" books leave off. Hunting can basically be divided into two segments, *getting the shot and making the shot*. This book fills the gap between your shooting and hunting skills. The bottom line is how you shoot when it really counts. To acquire this sometimes elusive ability, you must first understand how to get the most from yourself and your equipment.

The one issue that writers and bowhunters seem to neglect is what can be done before that once in a lifetime opportunity presents itself. The number is not important, but for a moment let's assume the average bowhunter will have 20 shot opportunities during his bowhunting career. If one bowhunter shoots accurately 10 percent of the time, he will affix a tag to just two animals in a lifetime. If another bowhunter shoots accurately 90 percent of the time, he will harvest 18 animals during his years of bowhunting. Also, this second bowhunter will almost certainly wound fewer animals in the process. This may be an oversimplification, but there is no need for you to make the same mistakes that have been made by thousands of other bowhunters countless times before.

At the beginning of my bowhunting career, I missed approximately 95 percent of my shots at game animals. Now, I estimate that over 90 percent of my shots are successful. That is a tremendous improvement, but it occurred over 30 years of trial and error. You might think that I just became a better shot with time, but that is not true. At the time I was doing much of the missing under hunting conditions, I held several Ohio State archery championships. On the target range, I was a better shot than I am today. What has changed over the years is my knowledge base and experience in all the other aspects of bowhunting.

Accurate shooting alone doesn't guarantee success when hunting. It is only one of many challenges that must be handled correctly when you are staring that big six-point bull in the eye and know you will only get one chance. Putting your arrow in the right spot during a situation like that requires more than just shooting ability. Buck fever, range estimation and trajectory can also cause you to miss that all-important shot. The weakest of these skills is often what determines your success or failure as a bowhunter.

The second portion of the book covers bowhunting equipment in detail. Some of the issues addressed are: high-energy cams, round wheel cams, fiberglass and wood limbs, metal and wood risers, feathers, vanes, release aids, sights, peep sights, bow strings, broadheads, etc. How do these items affect you? What are the advantages and disadvantages of each? Some of the answers may surprise you. Hopefully

you'll gain the knowledge to help you sort fact from fiction, whether you are choosing equipment or talking to other bowhunters or listening to a salesman. You should also come to understand how to apply this knowledge as you develop your own personalized strategy for bowhunting.

The reasons for a successful hunt are many, but the most important aspects are attitude, experience and knowledge. A proper attitude is developed and experience must be earned. But knowledge should be readily available to all who are willing to learn. The enjoyment of bowhunting goes far beyond the issues we will be discussing. The purpose of this book is to address certain issues, not to ignore others. As you read through the following pages, keep in mind that bowhunting is purely a personal sport. Many possible options and techniques will be discussed. You may decide that some alternatives take too much time or effort; others you just may not enjoy. To be able to choose what is best, however, you need to know and understand all of your options.

It took me many years of struggling to attain the skills necessary to harvest big animals consistently. The fall before starting this book I harvested six Pope and Young animals and a coyote with seven shots. Reaching that personal summit was well worth the effort. But it is my sincere desire that the road to *your* bowhunting goals will be shorter and less frustrating than mine. If the following chapters provide you with answers and a more direct route to bowhunting success, then I have accomplished my purpose.

Dave Holt
Denver, Colorado

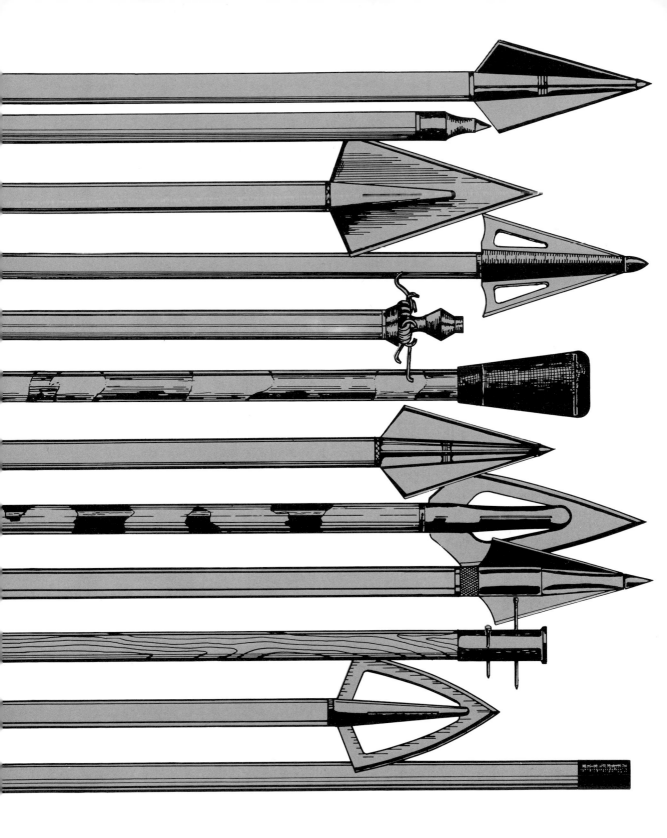

SHOOTING ABILITY 1

Shooting ability is certainly the foundation of successful bowhunting. For the purpose of this book, the term **shooting ability** is limited to how accurately you can shoot at targets with no outside disturbance or pressure. It is obvious that all tournament shooters are not successful bowhunters, but I have found that most consistently successful bowhunters are, at least, reasonably accurate shots. The few successful bowhunters who are not would be even more successful if they improved their shooting ability.

You often hear about the bowhunter who can't hit a target worth beans but is a fantastic game shot. Well, as G. Fred Asbell says in his book, *Instinctive Shooting,* "I don't believe a guy who can't hit the ground with a quiver full of arrows is going to be suddenly transformed into a crack shot because an animal came by. It just doesn't happen that way."

You don't necessarily need the ability to shoot arrow after arrow in a bull's-eye, but you do need the skill to put that first arrow where you want it to go. When a poor shooter is a consistently successful bowhunter, you can bet he is relying heavily on his other skills to provide many close-range shots.

Being able to consistently hold tight groups on paper targets isn't the complete answer either. As shared in the introduction, my early bowhunting years were generally unsuccessful, even though my shooting ability was above average and I had many excellent shots at game. Without strong shooting skills to build on, however, my road to success would have been longer and more difficult. Although its importance is paramount, shooting ability is only the first step to successful bowhunting.

This chapter is not intended to teach you step-by-step shooting basics or how to tune your bow. Those subjects have been well covered by authors such as Al Henderson, John Williams, G. Fred Asbell and Larry Wise, whose books will be mentioned later. The purpose of this chapter is to point out how shooting ability fits into the overall bowhunting picture.

You will also find ideas here on how to test your shooting skills and where to turn for help if your shooting ability needs to be improved. The information in the first five chapters of this book will assist you in evaluating your shooting skills and help you decide in what areas your efforts will be the most productive.

After releasing your very first arrow, you probably thought to yourself, "I'll never learn to shoot this antiquated excuse for a weapon." Like many new endeavors, getting started is the most difficult step. Don't give up! You'll be surprised how quickly your shooting ability will improve.

A combination of personal instruction, reading instructional archery material and experience (practice) is the quickest way to improve your shooting ability. Do not overlook any of these tools; they will all do their part to help you improve your shooting.

One summer, many years ago, a friend and I worked hard at perfecting our bowhunting skills, particularly our shooting skills. We were determined to harvest a large bull elk apiece, but like many hunting stories, it didn't turn out as we'd planned. As the last weekend of the season rolled around, we both still had unfilled elk tags. We decided at that late date any mature elk would be our target.

We weren't quite out of tricks because I knew a very interesting place to put our treestands. The massive old pine tree was perfect: about 40 feet up, it split in two and continued straight up. About five feet above the split, Ken and I placed our tree stands, directly across from each other. We both had a clear shot to the north, Ken could shoot to the west and I to the east. In addition, we could actually lean over and whisper to each other. Best of all, this was a place the elk loved to come. I had hunted the area for years and knew it well. It was very dependable for attracting cows and an occasional spike, though not big bulls.

We practiced shooting from the treestands as soon as they were placed. If the elk arrived as we hoped, there could be no excuses for errors in range estimation. This meant our shooting ability would play an important role in our success or failure.

It was about 5:00 a.m. Saturday morning when we climbed up the old pine to our stands. It would be light about 6:15. Even before it was light enough to see, we could hear elk moving below. Ken had won the coin toss for the first shot. As luck would have it, by legal shooting time, five cows were on my side of the tree. This did not present Ken with an opportunity to shoot; there was nothing we could do but wait.

It seemed like forever, but suddenly I saw Ken move as a large cow approached from his side of the tree. Ken nodded to me and I knew he was going to shoot. I took the opportunity to draw and aim at a large cow on my side of the tree. At the sound of Ken's shot, the elk scattered, without giving me enough time to shoot. But before entering the timber, the last cow stopped broadside about 30 yards away. I released my arrow, and she went crashing off through the thick spruce.

Our shots were within seconds of each other, and both of us felt we had good hits. About 30 minutes later, we climbed down. We found Ken's elk within 150 yards and mine was located 80 yards in the opposite direction. Two elk from the same tree within 10 seconds of each other! Our hard work and practice that summer had paid off with accurate shooting when it counted.

Many people can shoot accurately when the target is paper and they know the distance. The secret is making all your skills work together on those few shots that really count. Shooting ability is certainly an important skill, but only one of the many you must master to consistently put your first arrow in the right

place. Especially if the intended target is the biggest buck you've ever laid your eyes on.

Learning to shoot a bow can be a relaxing and enjoyable experience, but it can also be incredibly challenging and, at times, down-right frustrating. By limiting yourself to hunting with archery equipment, you put yourself on a more equal level with the animal. This presents an opportunity for greater challenge and personal satisfaction.

Often, a friend will be the one to get you involved in archery. That friend may also have a bow for sale. If you decide to purchase a used bow, make sure it is the correct draw weight and draw length for you. Also, (try to) make sure you pay a fair price. If you have any questions, this would be a good time to become familiar with your local pro shop. Don't make the mistake of buying a bow that is not right for you! Any reputable pro shop should be happy to help you with advice.

Reading on the subject of archery is an excellent way to increase your knowledge of shooting techniques and bowhunting in general. While this book is not an instructional shooting book, it certainly will give you ideas on how to improve both your equipment and your shooting skills. It will also help you to make more intelligent choices about equipment you may want to purchase and about the type of practice that will benefit you the most. This book is intended to pick up where the instructional shooting books leave off.

Before you start shooting, or trying to improve your shooting ability, read at least one good instructional book. The following books will help improve your shooting techniques:

Understanding Winning Archery,
by Al Henderson.
Archery for Beginners,
by John Williams.

If you shoot instinctively, I recommend *Instinctive Shooting,* by G. Fred Asbell. If you shoot a compound bow, I recommend *Tuning Your Compound Bow,* by Larry Wise. *Bowhunting with Easton Aluminum Arrow Shafts* also offers some excellent bow tuning tips. This handy little booklet is free from your local pro shop or from Easton Aluminum (5040 W. Harold Gatty Dr., Salt Lake City, Utah 84116-2897). In addition, many archery companies offer good, free, pocket-size instructional books.

The best place to locate the books you are interested in is at your local pro shop. If they don't stock the book you are looking for, ask them to order it for you. Many pro shops also offer personal instruction. If you are a beginner, in a rut, or have a problem, this could be a viable solution. Make sure you get an experienced instructor. The National Field Archery Association has a certified archery instructor program. Don't be afraid to ask if your instructor has completed this program.

A very good investment is a subscription to at least one good archery periodical. *Bowhunter Magazine* is an excellent choice; it offers good hunting stories, keeps you informed on issues and gives you various state-to-state reports on upcoming seasons. Personally, I find even the advertisements interesting. They keep me up to date on new products I may want to try and provide information about where to find items that are not offered locally.

Your local library is an additional source of archery reading material. Local bookstores are another possibility. A book reference list, with publishers' addresses, has also been provided at the back of this text to help you locate other instructional reading material.

Once you have your equipment and basic instruction, the best way to improve your ability is with continuous and diligent practice. Set your goal for quality not quantity; just shooting arrow after arrow is not the answer. Think through each shot. Become familiar with what a good-shot "feels" like and be able to diagnose a poor shot. And don't forget to continue your practice throughout the season.

It is also a good idea to shoot at a local club or range. These are excellent places to meet others who are interested in bowhunting. Meeting other bowhunters, making new friends, discussing past and future hunts and gaining and sharing knowledge are all enjoyable parts of our sport. Like any gathering of fishermen or hunters, though, there'll be a need for caution on your part as to what is accepted as factual. Most of the time, the person sharing some bit of information really believes it to be the truth and certainly means no harm. But there is a danger in accepting incorrect information as the gospel. If what you have been told is false, it may take you years of experience to find out the truth, and who knows what it will cost you along the way!

As an example, I would like to tell on a close friend. His name has been changed to protect the guilty. For a little background information, George has 35 years of hunting experience. He is an excellent shot and has harvested over 50 big game animals with a rifle and five with the bow. Just so you don't think the following occurred because George is not very bright, he holds a doctoral degree and is well respected in his field.

George arrived at the hunting area a day ahead of me and had harvested a deer that first evening. I arrived early the next afternoon and was quickly told the story several times over. It went like this. George went to his treestand early, as usual. Late in the afternoon, a doe approached to within 20 yards. George missed with his first arrow because of the infamous unseen tree limb. Fortunately, the doe moved only a few yards and presented an excellent "quartering away" shot. The second arrow appeared to hit perfectly and the deer traveled only 20 yards before collapsing.

George had the field-dressed doe tagged and in his truck ready to head for home when I arrived the next day. Because of my strong interest in shot placement and how far animals travel after being hit, I asked George if I could remove the deer from the truck and examine the entrance and exit wounds. George agreed and as I raised a hind leg to help remove the doe from the truck, I immediately noticed that the deer was a buck.

After giving George a good razzing, I continued to check the button buck. George's "quartering away" shot had entered the deer's hindquarter a half-inch left of where the tail bone attaches to the body and the exit hole was at mid-rib cage on the right side. Hardly a "quartering away" shot. The first shot that George had thought was a miss had hit the deer high at the base of the neck causing a nonfatal injury. George had not noticed this wound. None of the misinformation in George's story was intentional. He honestly believed he was telling the facts as they happened—until I pointed out the evidence conflicting with his story.

When an animal is harvested, the potential for learning is tremendous. For George, the learning stopped just after he released his last arrow. I must admit George has been a good sport through all the kidding but more importantly he has agreed to the following: he will keep accurate records, including checking the internal organs closely to see exactly what was hit; he will never assume what organs were struck unless he recovers the animal and checks internally; he will use only personal observations when compiling his records. This is good advice for everyone and will help many bowhunters gain valuable knowledge that is often overlooked. Oh yes, George has also agreed to correctly determine the sex of the animal prior to filling out his game tag.

Believing George's story as it was originally told would not hurt anyone other than George, but it does show how quickly the facts can become confused. My advice is to be extremely observant when you are personally involved. If someone tells you something that doesn't sound right, ask questions and get several knowledgeable opinions. Above all, use good, old-fashioned common sense in all hunting situations.

SHOOTING POSITIONS

Shooting positions and their effects on accuracy vary widely from shooter to shooter. Some shooters suffer disastrous effects if they change position even slightly, while others can seemingly shoot standing on their heads and not be affected.

A point to keep in mind is that changes in your shooting form often have a greater effect on your accuracy than shooting up or downhill. Shooting from different angles may affect the point of impact of the arrow. But I believe the biggest culprits are changes in shooting form and misjudging distances. Shooting at targets from above or below can affect your draw length, anchor point, back tension, release or head angle. The natural assumption might be to blame the angle of the shot when an arrow hits high or low. As near as possible, always try to keep your upper body in a normal shooting position. This is good advice any time you attempt a shot from an unnatural position.

Regardless of the causes or results, it would be foolish for any of us not to practice from a variety of shooting positions, including up- and downhill. If you plan to hunt from treestands, include them in your practice before the season opens. Also learn how low you can crouch and shoot without the bottom limb of your bow hitting the ground. In tight or rushed shooting situations, be aware of nearby obstacles such as a log that might be struck by your lower limb or a nearby branch that, by being so close, doesn't appear in your line of sight.

The main point for practicing ahead of time is to prevent a little subtlety from costing you the trophy of a lifetime. Although, believe me, when a lesson is learned in a situation like that, it is not soon forgotten.

SHOOTING DISTANCE

Regardless of your experience level, you must consider the distance from which you attempt shots at game animals. This is often referred to as your **maximum effective range**. Many instructors and writers will set the same limit for all bowhunters without considering individual shooting ability. This approach does make the excellent point that we must all place restrictions on ourselves and limit our shooting distance while hunting.

From my observations under hunting conditions, shooting accuracy is too wide ranging to put an arbitrary limit on all bowhunters' maximum effective range. We should all find our own individual maximum effective range before the season opens. A simple test will help you find the maximum distance you should attempt a shot at an animal.

To test yourself, set up a normal 8-inch paper plate for a target (figure 1). Then find the maximum distance from which you can consistently hit the plate, five out of five shots. This distance or less should be considered your maximum effective range for deer. The distance at which you intend to limit your shots should be individually determined and set in your mind before you hunt. Dealing with brush, wind, low light conditions, terrain changes and buck fever are the realities of hunting. These obstacles have the potential to affect your shooting ability, so always make your maximum range a conservative estimate. If you consistently miss shots while hunting, shorten the

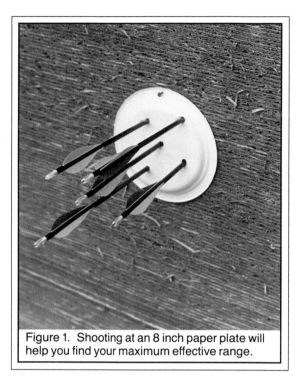

Figure 1. Shooting at an 8 inch paper plate will help you find your maximum effective range.

distance you have set as your maximum effective range.

Your average group size is another useful tool for finding your maximum effective range. A group, usually three to five arrows, is measured in a straight line from the inside to the inside of the two shafts in the group that are the greatest distance apart. Regardless of the shooter or the beginning group size, the group enlarges at a consistent rate as the range increases. An important point to remember is that as the distance of the shot increases, so will the group size and *both by the same percentage*.

All you need for a starting point is your average group size at a set distance, as illustrated in the group enlargement table on the next page. To determine your group size, shoot five five-shot groups, measure and record the size of each group. Add the figures from the group sizes together and divide by 5 to deter-

Group Enlargement Table

The beginning distances and group sizes are:

25 yards = 2.0 - inch group

30 yards = 2.4 - inch group
35 yards = 2.8 - inch group
40 yards = 3.2 - inch group
45 yards = 3.6 - inch group
50 yards = 4.0 - inch group

25 yards = 5.0 - inch group

30 yards = 6.0 - inch group
35 yards = 7.0 - inch group
40 yards = 8.0 - inch group
45 yards = 9.0 - inch group
50 yards = 10.0 - inch group

25 yards = 3.0 - inch group

30 yards = 3.6 - inch group
35 yards = 4.2 - inch group
40 yards = 4.8 - inch group
45 yards = 5.4 - inch group
50 yards = 6.0 - inch group

25 yards = 6.0 - inch group

30 yards = 7.2 - inch group
35 yards = 8.4 - inch group
40 yards = 9.6 - inch group
45 yards = 10.8 - inch group
50 yards = 12.0 - inch group

25 yards = 4.0 - inch group

30 yards = 4.8 - inch group
35 yards = 5.6 - inch group
40 yards = 6.4 - inch group
45 yards = 7.2 - inch group
50 yards = 8.0 - inch group

25 yards = 7.0 - inch group

30 yards = 8.4 - inch group
35 yards = 9.8 - inch group
40 yards = 11.2 - inch group
45 yards = 12.6 - inch group
50 yards = 14.0 - inch group

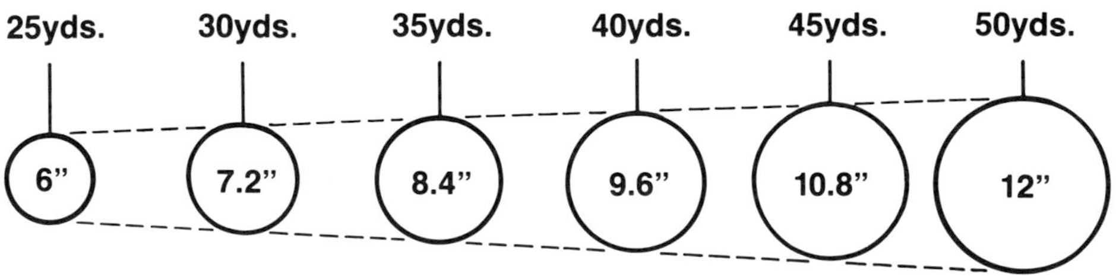

25yds.	30yds.	35yds.	40yds.	45yds.	50yds.
6"	7.2"	8.4"	9.6"	10.8"	12"

The group size enlarges as the range increases.

mine the average group size. The information below will help make this process more clear.

For this example, the yardage and group size have been increased 20 percent each time. Let's assume your average group size was 6 inches at 25 yards; 20 percent of these figures convert to 5 yards in distance, and 1.2 inches in group size. By adding these numbers to your beginning group size and distance you now know approximately what your group size should be. If you wish to find information not listed in the table, simply find your group size at a set distance then increase the group size and the distance by the same percentage.

At 50 yards, you simply doubled the group size because the distance was doubled. You could continue this process to determine your average group size at any distance you would like. You could reverse the process and reduce the group size as you decrease the distance.

For an accurate test, your arrows must be exactly the same in all respects. Then, if your groups do not follow this pattern, the cause could be a tuning problem with the bow or a slight inconsistency in your shooting form. One factor the above information does not allow for is a change in arrow speed. Most shooters have some fluctuation in arrow speed because of a slight variation in their draw length and release. Because of these variables, it is not advisable to concern yourself with a departure from the above formula of less than 5 percent.

Some may think the above method is complicated. It really is not. You need only a pencil, paper and small measuring tape to record your group sizes. Now, you ask, "What do I do with the information once it is collected?" This information can be used to help with the following:

- It gets you more involved with your shooting and helps you keep track of your progress from season to season.

- After finding your average group size at 25 yards, the formula can help you determine if you are shooting more accurately at one distance than another.

- It helps you understand how the natural enlargement of a group occurs as the range increases.

- It helps you find your average group size for any distance you like without actually shooting that distance. This information can then be used as another method to help you decide the maximum distance at which you should attempt a shot at a given species of big game animal.

For this new analysis of your shooting ability to be of help in the field, you need to know the average vital area size of the animal or animals you intend to hunt. With information supplied by Dr. Gordon Soloman of the University of Colorado, shot placement instructor, Shari Fraker, and my own field measurements from harvested big game animals, I have arrived at the following circular size vital areas: elk—12 inches, deer—8 inches, and antelope—6 inches, as depicted in figure number 2 on the next page.

The above numbers represent the broadside vital area of a mature male animal from each species listed. The size of the vital area will change with the maturity and sex of the individual animal. Penetrating this area with a razor sharp broadhead from the broadside position will ensure a quick, humane harvest of the animal.

The vital area described is located in the chest, directly behind the front shoulder, reaching from the third to the seventh rib. Vertically, it is located below center mass and drops to within a few inches of the bottom of the chest. There are certainly other areas and shot angles

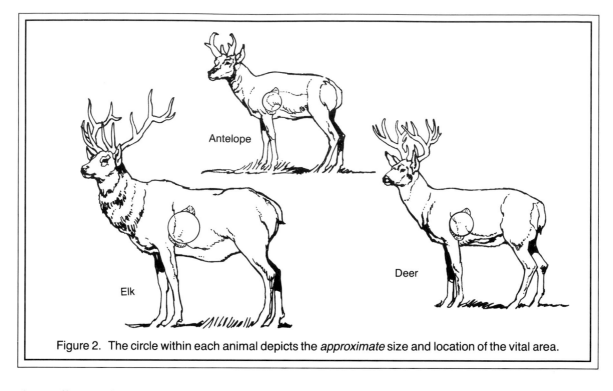

Figure 2. The circle within each animal depicts the *approximate* size and location of the vital area.

that will provide a quick humane kill. This, however, is the largest single area of the animal's anatomy that will ensure success on a consistent basis. The size of this area on the animal you intend to hunt will give you a target size to relate to your shooting ability.

Several years ago, my shooting ability was the primary factor in a successful elk hunt. While scouting, I located a heavily used meadow and wallow area. It was obvious from the amount of sign that the elk visited the meadow daily. I put up a treestand, but the wind always gave me away and the elk would never come within bow range. After reevaluating the situation, I realized that my only option—because of the wind—was a tree located exactly 50 yards from the main trail. After putting my stand in that tree and taking plenty of practice shots, I realized I could make the shot to the trail every time. The next morning, a bull was kind enough to stop at the exact spot where I had

been practicing. The result was a perfect broadside, double-lung shot with complete penetration. The bull traveled less than 100 yards.

No shot at an animal should be attempted, regardless of the distance, unless you are confident of your ability to harvest that animal humanely. There are times, however, as in the above example, when you may have the opportunity to test your ability before the moment of truth. Personally, I would prefer a 40-yard shot that I have had the opportunity to practice ahead of time, over a 30-yard shot where I am forced to estimate the range.

SHOOTING ACCURACY

If an average bowhunter with two years' experience could draw, aim where he wanted and for as long as he liked, then release smoothly, his shooting accuracy would surpass 90 percent of the bowhunters afield. Why does this seemingly simple task become so difficult once the basic fundamentals of shooting are mastered? Al Henderson, former U.S. Olympic coach, says the problem is fear. I concur and believe this fear is the fear of missing.

Although the mechanics of shooting must be learned and consistently followed, the bow and arrow is not a difficult weapon to master. There is a catch, and that is buck fever or target panic. Buck fever or target panic mentally prevents many archers from completing the shot with good shooting form. If you are not comfortable with the term buck fever or target panic, call it freezing, flinching, snap shooting or whatever else you like. Regardless of the term, be aware that it's there, it's real, and it's "public enemy number one" for the bowhunter when it comes to accurate shooting of the bow and arrow. Bowhunters must be aware that target panic or buck fever can have disastrous effects on their ability to complete each shot with proper shooting form. Methods for controlling buck fever will be discussed in detail in a later chapter.

A common mistake many bowhunters make is shooting too many arrows each time while practicing. This can make fingers and muscles sore. It can also get you thinking in terms of a quiverfull rather than the individual arrow. When you are practicing, think in terms of quality not quantity. In other words, don't overdo the number of arrows you shoot. Try to practice more often but shoot fewer arrows each time. Shoot each arrow as if it were your first one and your last. In hunting situations, that will probably be the case.

As you work to improve your shooting ability, it is imperative to identify the cause of inaccurate shooting. This is an important step to correcting a problem. Once again, reading, competent instructions and proper practice are the tools you should use to build upon your shooting ability.

In reading the next few chapters, it may appear that I do not consider shooting ability important. For the record, I do consider a bowhunter's shooting skills to be of prime importance. The point I will be making is to guard against over practicing in one area while neglecting another of equal importance to successful bowhunting. But if you are the fellow who can shoot the eyes out of a snake don't feel guilty and let your skill go unrewarded. Accurate shooting at hunting camp can keep you from doing the dishes, if you play your cards right! And remember it works best if you make up the rules.

TRAJECTORY 2

Arrow trajectory, as it relates to bowhunting, has long been a favorite subject of mine. It has been interesting to find that the general bowhunting public considers penetration more important than trajectory. Recently, that trend has been changing. How you deal with the problem of trajectory, like most aspects of bowhunting, is another personal choice. But before you can make that choice, you need accurate information. Three engineers have graciously donated their time in assisting me with compiling the information offered in this text. Thanks to the generosity of Norb Mullaney, Larry J. Luterman and Mike Gordon, I am able to offer this information for your consideration.

Trajectory is defined as the curve, or arc, in the flight path of the arrow as it moves from the bow to its first point of impact. If trajectory is "reduced," the flight path of the arrow will become straighter (flatter), with less curve or arc. The faster an arrow moves, the less curve or arc there is in its trajectory and the less the arrow drops as it moves toward the target.

Flattened trajectory is extremely beneficial. It should be made clear, however, that stability, accuracy, arrow flight and bow dependability should be maintained at all times. If you are interested in flattening trajectory, it is important to maintain these elements, as the arrow speed is increased.

As more precise arrow ballistics information has been made available, the positive attributes of a fast-moving arrow have become obvious. For the sake of illustration, we will compare a 500-grain arrow with a 600-grain arrow shot from the same bow. The 500-grain arrow can exhibit 16 percent less drop in trajectory. The trajectory is flattened because the lighter arrow leaves the bow at a higher rate of speed. But the 600-grain arrow delivers approximately 2½ percent more kinetic energy than the 500-grain arrow. The amount of kinetic energy delivered by an arrow is what affects penetration. This information assumes that the draw weight or draw length of the bow has not been changed. Here's how it works.

Reducing the weight of the arrow by 100 grains flattens its trajectory by approximately 16 percent while only reducing the arrow's ability to penetrate by about 2½ percent. So, we have gained 16 percent of a critical element and given up 2½ percent of an element usually not as critical when using hunting weight bows. If you are concerned with the 2½ percent reduction in kinetic energy, you would need to add only 2 pounds in draw weight to regain this loss. This action would also reduce the trajectory another 3 percent for a total reduction of about 19 percent.

For those who have the physical ability, trajectory can be reduced substantially by adding draw weight. If you increase the draw weight of your bow by 10 pounds, without any other changes, it will have the following effect. Trajectory will be reduced or flattened by approximately 17 percent and kinetic energy will be increased by about 14 percent. Keep in mind that when the draw weight is increased, the bow may require a stiffer arrow shaft. Increasing the "spine" (stiffness) of the shaft does not automatically increase the physical weight. This subject will be discussed later in this chapter and more thoroughly in the chapter on "Arrows."

Since percentages do not mean as much as an example, I will show how the above data would affect you in a hunting situation. If you attempted a shot at a deer that you estimated to be 30 yards away, and the actual distance to the deer was 33 yards (assuming you made a perfect shot in all other respects), the following would occur: With an arrow leaving the bow at 180 feet per second (FPS), you would completely miss the deer; but with an arrow leaving the bow at 220 FPS, you would harvest the deer.

There is another benefit to arrow speed that I find most intriguing. During the '50s, '60s and '70s, I was all too aware of the possibility of animals "jumping the string." This occurs when the animal has enough time to move from the path of the arrow, causing the shot to be missed. Recent slow-motion footage shows that some deer actually drop toward the ground and at the same time start turning as they attempt to jump the string. The animal may be reacting to either the movement or sound of the bow upon release, and at longer ranges, the sight or sound of the arrow moving through the air. Even with the use of string silencers, this happened to me many times and it was always frustrating. Slowly, I became aware that the animals, at very close range, had a more difficult time jumping the string. As the range increased, it became more likely that this phenomenon would occur.

During the early '80s, I slowly increased my arrow speed to about 230 FPS. Since that time, I have not had one animal jump the string at distances under 30 yards. The reason, quite simply, was the arrow speed. So I investigated this possibility and came up with the following information. An arrow moving 180 FPS will travel 29 yards in one-half of a second. An arrow moving 240 FPS will travel 39 yards in that same one-half second. That is over 30 percent farther in the same amount of time (figure 3). This additional arrow speed reduces the possibility that an animal will jump the string (figures 4A & B). Apparently the time required for an arrow traveling 230 FPS to reach an animal at distances under 30 yards is less than the *average* animal's reaction time.

Penetration is a very controversial subject and consequently has long been a concern of bowhunters. As previously stated, if you reduce your arrow weight 100 grains, you lose only about 2½ percent in kinetic energy (penetrating ability). This loss is minimal when weighed against the reduction in trajectory. Penetration is affected far more by arrow flight than it is by arrow weight. This relationship is difficult to

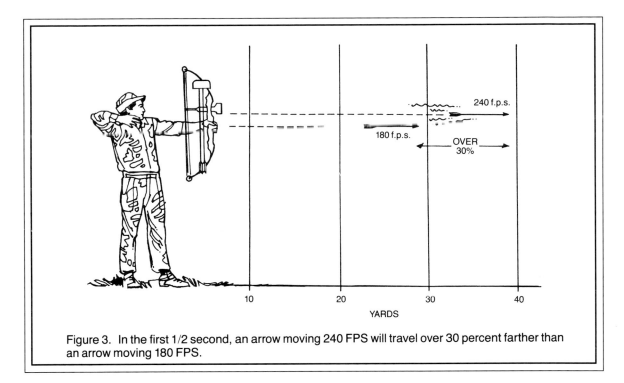

Figure 3. In the first 1/2 second, an arrow moving 240 FPS will travel over 30 percent farther than an arrow moving 180 FPS.

Figure 4A. When animals "jump the string" they often drop and turn from the flight path of the arrow.

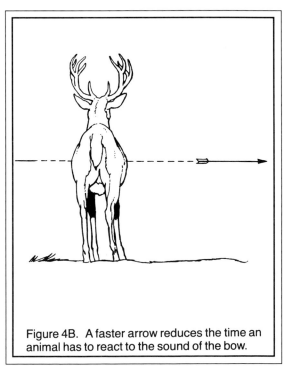

Figure 4B. A faster arrow reduces the time an animal has to react to the sound of the bow.

actually measure, but imperfect arrow flight can have serious negative effects on penetration.

The following situation alerted me to the fact that arrow flight definitely affects penetration. Several years ago, I was shooting a heavy bow, 75 pounds, and heavy arrows, 2219s. The bow had a solid shelf with mohair for an arrow rest. I could not get the arrows to fly perfectly but was able to shoot 5-inch groups with the bow at 30 yards. This was very good for me so I was not that concerned with the imperfect arrow flight.

While hunting with that bow for two years and taking several big game animals, including mule deer, whitetail deer, elk, mountain goat and mountain lion, it became evident that my arrow penetration was less than most of my hunting partners'. While they often achieved complete penetration of the animal, I seldom got an exit wound even on deer. This did not cause a problem as far as losing an animal was concerned. With that bow, I had a string of six animals collapse within sight.

Due to the wear on my feathers, I decided to change to a different style of arrow rest (for complete information on this rest, see the chapter on "Accessories"). My new rest provided excellent arrow flight, and that season I noticed a marked improvement in penetration. This was surprising because I had also changed to a lighter arrow, slightly reducing the kinetic energy. Theoretically this should have reduced penetration, but instead, it was increased. The only logical explanation was the improved arrow flight.

Here's another experience that drew my attention to the effects of arrow flight on penetration. A few years ago, a friend's wife shot a mule deer buck while she hunted from one of my treestands. The buck was standing 30 yards away, in a quartering away position, when Cheryl released her arrow. The shot was perfect. The arrow struck two ribs and still passed

completely through the buck. The penetration was so impressive I took the opportunity to examine the situation closely. Cheryl's equipment included a 42-pound, round wheel compound bow and a 400-grain arrow with a replaceable blade broadhead. The only contributing cause I could find for such tremendous penetration with light equipment was the perfect arrow flight.

From these and other personal experiences, it is evident to me that arrow flight affects penetration much more than arrow weight. My observations show that very poor arrow flight can affect penetration dramatically. As mentioned earlier, to accurately measure the effect of arrow flight on penetration is very difficult. Regardless, it is indisputable that penetration will be adversely affected by a wobbling arrow. The only question is how much it will be affected. Most bowhunters blame poor penetration on arrow weight or broadhead design. In many cases, I am convinced the real culprit is arrow flight (figure 5).

My observations in the field have shown that a surprising number of bowhunters have arrow flight problems. Some reasons for imperfect arrow flight are the lack of knowledge about bow tuning, a poor release, and the use of very large broadheads. Other factors that can affect arrow flight are the bow string hitting bulky clothes, the arrow striking twigs or brush, and buck fever.

Vane-fletched arrows do not, by themselves, cause arrow flight problems. They are, however, more sensitive to existing problems than are feathered arrows under the same conditions.

In other words, if you have an arrow flight problem, it will generally become more severe if you shoot vane-fletched arrows. For more information on correcting arrow flight problems, see *Tuning Your Compound Bow,* by Larry Wise.

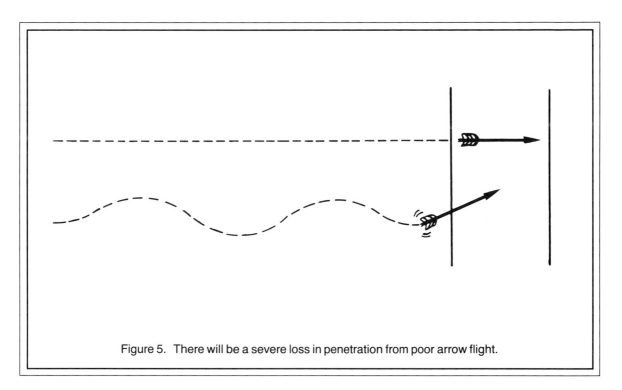

Figure 5. There will be a severe loss in penetration from poor arrow flight.

UNDERSTANDING TRAJECTORY

A 30-06 rifle, properly sighted-in, will hit a deer from zero to approximately 250 yards without concern about trajectory or sighting over the intended target. But the average big game animal harvested in the United States with a rifle is shot at less than 100 yards. Despite this fact, there have been many articles written regarding the values of flat rifle trajectory. Rifle shooters will discuss for hours the attributes of a flat shooting rifle and in general are well versed on the subject.

Yet a bowhunter, using an average hunting bow and arrow combination, holding his 20-yard sight pin dead-on where he hopes to hit the target, can only kill a deer-size big game animal out to approximately 25 yards. Beyond this distance he would miss because of trajectory alone, regardless of his ability to shoot accurately. This is due solely to the tremendous amount of trajectory inherent even in modern archery equipment.

Considering all the elements, the bowhunter must be far more concerned with trajectory than the rifle hunter. Many of today's bowhunters, however, believe that arrow weight (penetration) is more important than arrow speed (trajectory) in regard to harvesting an animal. As hunters, we should understand how trajectory affects us in a hunting situation, regardless of our choice of weapons.

It is impossible to eliminate trajectory entirely from the flight path of an arrow by changing your archery equipment. But my ultimate objective is to take what the bow and arrow has to offer as a weapon and make it work in the most efficient manner possible. Shooting a fast arrow does not mean you can expect to hit every animal that presents a shot opportunity. You must still be very concerned with range estimation.

Check the trajectory chart provided at the end of this chapter and you will see that an arrow moving 240 FPS has over 46 percent less trajectory than an arrow moving at 180 FPS. Shooting at unknown distances, the arrow moving 240 FPS, allows you almost twice the margin for error in range estimation as would the arrow moving 180 FPS. Reducing the trajectory path of your arrow increases the amount of error you can make when estimating the distance to an animal (figure 6). Thus the chance of wounding an animal is minimized. This fact alone makes the effort well worthwhile.

As explained in the previous chapter, a mature deer offers only about an 8-inch vital area. This is the largest circular area available directly to the rear of the front shoulder bone. There are certainly other areas that will provide a quick, humane harvest of the animal; however, this is the largest single area of the animal's anatomy that will ensure success on a consistent basis. The important fact here is that if you shoot for the center of this vital area, you have only a 4-inch margin for error in all directions. With this information, it is a simple matter to look at the trajectory chart and see how much error in range estimation it takes for an arrow moving a certain speed to fall 4 inches.

As you can see, arrow speed alone will not solve all range estimation problems. It is, however, another building block in the foundation of the successful bowhunter. A fast arrow will help you humanely harvest the animal that would have been wounded or missed by a narrow margin. A fast arrow will only be helpful with high and low shots. It will not help if you shoot to the right or left of your target.

Even though I was aware of how trajectory affects the bowhunter, one cold November morning in 1985 the point was brought home hard once again. The temperature stood at a

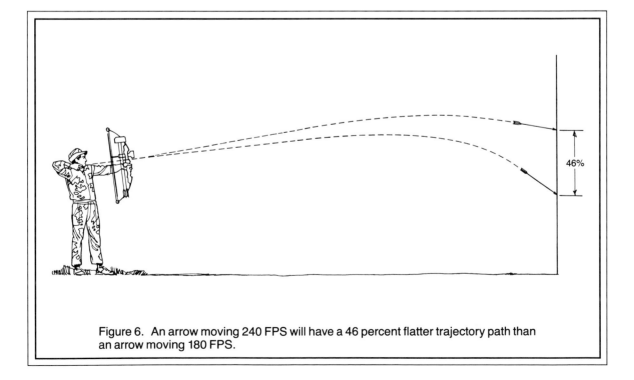

Figure 6. An arrow moving 240 FPS will have a 46 percent flatter trajectory path than an arrow moving 180 FPS.

cold 10 degrees and a strong, northwest wind pelted me with icy snow crystals as I stood shivering in my treestand. As I seriously considered giving up for the morning, a large whitetail buck appeared, working a scrape line in my direction. After waiting as long as possible to remove the heavy glove from my shooting hand, I took the bow, with the arrow nocked, from its hanging place in the tree. Just out of range, the buck decided to make a new scrape. My fingers were numb and the possibility of freezing to death seemed very real. Finally, the buck moved on, then stopped broadside in a lane directly in front of me. Placing my 30-yard pin just behind his front shoulder, in the middle of the vital area, I released my arrow. The shot felt good but my heart sank. The arrow had good line but the hit looked high. As the buck bounded away, I was a little uncertain about the hit.

To confirm the yardage, I shot all my blunts to where the buck had been standing and determined that 25 yards—not 30 yards—would have been a much more accurate estimate of the distance. To keep from freezing, I needed to move while waiting to track the buck. For something to do, I went to my truck, picked up my measuring tape and returned to the treestand. Using the measuring tape, the distance from the tree to the buck's tracks proved to be 26 yards.

It was finally time to track the buck. As I started off on a light bloodtrail, I wondered if a 4 yard error in range estimation would cost me the biggest whitetail buck of my hunting career. A little less than 200 yards later, a large antler protruding from the grass removed my doubts and lifted my spirits to a new high. As I looked down at a beautiful Pope and Young buck, I was thankful that I had done everything possible to flatten the trajectory path of my arrows.

An internal check of the buck's vital organs revealed that the arrow had entered just under the backbone. Because of the downward angle of the shot, the arrow sliced through the top of the off-side lung before exiting and the buck died quickly. Had I been using a slower bow, one with more arrow trajectory, I may have wounded or missed this buck completely.

IMPROVING TRAJECTORY

If you are interested in flattening trajectory, you must increase arrow speed. The following information shows how each change will help you accomplish that goal.

1. Arrow speed will increase approximately 4 FPS for each 25-grain reduction in arrow weight. This figure is an average for hunting weight arrows.
2. Arrow speed will increase approximately 1¾ FPS for each pound of draw weight that is added.

Considering these facts, let's take an average bowhunter and see what improvements can be made.

Ken is shooting an inefficient, round wheel compound bow set at 55 pounds. His draw length is 30 inches; his arrow is a 2020 with a 150-grain broadhead. The total arrow weight is over 620 grains and his bow shoots this arrow at 170 FPS.

Ken reads this book and decides he wants as much arrow speed as possible. He works hard and is finally able to shoot his bow comfortably with the draw weight set at 65 pounds. He makes a wise choice of arrow size with the 2215 and chooses a 125-grain broadhead. His arrow weight is now about 520 grains for the 65-pound bow. Ken has now gained approximately 18 FPS from the added bow weight and 16 FPS for the arrow weight reduction. Ken's bow now shoots the 520-grain arrow at 204

FPS and he has reduced the trajectory path of his arrow by over 33 percent.

By reducing the trajectory path of his arrow, Ken increases his allowable margin for error when shooting targets or animals at unknown yardages. It works like this. The more you flatten the flight path of the arrow, the more you can misjudge the distance and still hit your target. The amount that Ken flattens the trajectory path of his arrow is the exact amount that his margin for error will increase. If Ken's old equipment allows for a 3-yard margin for error and he reduces his trajectory by 33 percent, which in this case equals 1 yard, he would increase his allowable margin for error to 4 yards. See the table below.

Here's how it would work in the field. Ken is about to attempt a shot at an elk he believes is standing at a distance of 30 yards. Before flattening the trajectory path of his arrow, Ken could kill the elk if it were actually standing between 27 and 33 yards away from him, a margin of error of only 3 yards in each direction from 30 yards. After reducing his trajectory by 33 percent, Ken would have a 4-yard margin for error in each direction from 30 yards. Now he could kill the elk if it were standing between 26 and 34 yards away from him. By reducing the trajectory 33 percent, Ken adds 1 yard in each direction to his allowable margin for error (figure 7). There are two ways to look at this information. You can say that 2 yards total is not enough distance to make a difference. On the other hand, you can say that 33 percent is a tremendous improvement. Personally, I prefer the latter, knowing it will help me hit animals more cleanly at unknown distances.

The above information was used only as an example. In reality, it is not 100-percent technically correct because an arrow drops more rapidly after passing the distance it was intended to strike a given target. In other words, an arrow is dropping more during the first few yards beyond the distance it was shot for than it is the few yards prior to reaching that distance. You might recall a time when your arrow was headed right for the target and at the last instant it dropped low. For example, if your arrow speed gives you a 5-yard margin for error at 30 yards, in reality, those 5 yards would fall more closely between 27 and 32 yards than they would between 27½ and 32½ as the example in Ken's story would indicate.

The above improvements in trajectory are realistic and obtainable for most bowhunters. Bows, however, do vary considerably in arrow speed, and this fact must be allowed for in each situation (see the chapter on "The Bow at Work").

As stated earlier, the lighter the arrow, the faster it moves, thus the flatter its trajectory. Arrows are matched to bows by stiffness or spine, not by physical weight. Easton Aluminum Company marks the shaft size on each

Ken's Equipment

Before	After
Draw Weight - 55#	Draw Weight - 65#
Draw Length - 30"	Draw Length - 30"
Arrow Shaft Size - 2020	Arrow Shaft Size - 2215
Broadhead Weight - 150	Broadhead Weight - 125
Total Arrow Weight - 620	Total Arrow Weight - 520
Arrow Speed - 170	Arrow Speed - 204

Ken's improvement in arrow speed.

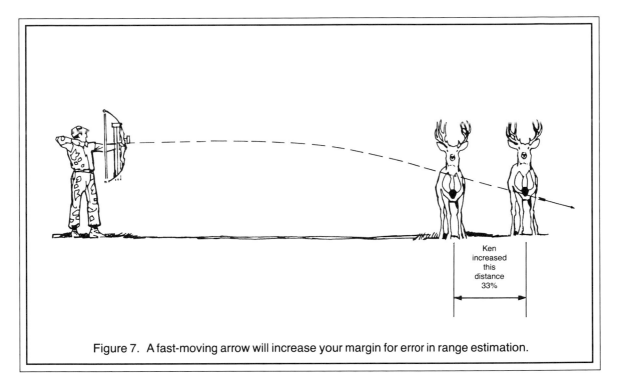

Figure 7. A fast-moving arrow will increase your margin for error in range estimation.

arrow in number form. The first number indicates the outside diameter of the shaft in 64ths of an inch. The second number indicates the thickness of the shaft wall in thousandths. An example of this would be a 2117 shaft, which is $^{21}/_{64}$ of an inch in diameter and has a wall thickness of $^{17}/_{1000}$ of an inch (figure 8).

The shaft sizes that provide the highest spine for the least amount of physical weight are the 2013, 2114, 2213, 2215, 2312, 2314, 2413 and the 2512. For example, Easton's latest hunting shaft selection chart lists both the 2020 and the 2213 as choices for a 60-pound, 30-inch draw length compound bow. These two shafts are just over 100 grains apart in physical weight. A 30-inch 2314 is approximately 23 grains lighter than a 30-inch 2216, but the spine is approximately the same. A 2117 and 2216 are the same physical weight, but the 2216 has a heavier spine. These examples show that there are often options that can reduce the total arrow

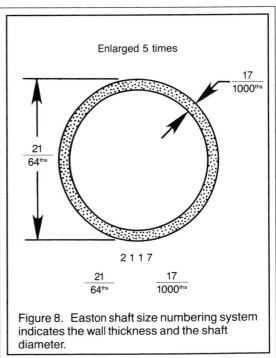

Figure 8. Easton shaft size numbering system indicates the wall thickness and the shaft diameter.

weight.

By choosing the correct arrow size, you can reduce arrow weight without reducing spine, or increase spine without increasing arrow weight. Personally, I do not like to shoot arrow sizes over ¹¹⁄₃₂ or ²²⁄₆₄ of an inch in diameter. My draw length of 29¾ inches is short enough that I can get away with this, even when shooting heavy bows. Check Easton's chart for their recommendations as to your draw weight and draw length.

One fact you might like to be aware of is that an insert for a 2215 shaft weighs 28 grains and an insert for a 2315 shaft weighs 48 grains. All shaft sizes above ¹¹⁄₃₂ of an inch would follow this pattern. This is a result of the extra metal required to taper down to the typical broadhead size, which is ¹¹⁄₃₂ of an inch in diameter. A good portion of the insert weight can be eliminated by choosing Easton Aluminum's new carbon inserts. See the chapter on "Arrows."

Before leaving the subject of trajectory, I would once again like to make it very clear that stability, accuracy, arrow flight and bow dependability are more important than arrow speed. This also includes not "over-bowing" yourself (too much draw weight). I have found that most active men can shoot 60 to 80 pounds when using a round wheel compound bow with a 50-percent let-off. Most active women can handle 40 to 55 pounds. Personally, I like a few pounds less draw weight when I shoot a modified or high-energy cam bow.

If you are not as concerned about trajectory as you are about penetration, do yourself a favor. Keep track of how many animals you lose due to a lack of penetration versus those you miss because you either shot over or under the animal. Keeping track of these situations will assist you in making an honest evaluation of the importance of trajectory as it relates to your hunting style. Reducing trajectory is something you can do ahead of time to help increase your chances for success in hunting situations.

TRAJECTORY TABLE

The information for this table was determined by using 2216 arrows with broadheads. The total arrow weight is 560 grains. Three 5-inch feathers were also used on the arrows with a mild helical fletch. If you use a different arrow weight or style fletching, any change in trajectory (drop of the arrow) will be minimal for normal hunting weight arrows. Most hunting arrows weigh between 450 and 650 grains. All you need to know is your initial arrow speed.

The table is designed to tell you, at a glance, how low your arrow will strike when you underjudge the distance to a target by 5 yards. For example, a deer stops broadside; you quickly estimate the distance to be 25 yards and aim accordingly. Carefully holding in the center of the vital area, you release your arrow. The arrow looks low because the deer was actually standing 30 yards away. A mature deer has an 8-inch vital area. If you properly sighted in the center of the kill area there was only a 4-inch margin for error, high or low. Assuming you made an accurate shot, did you harvest the deer? If your arrow speed was less than 220 FPS, you missed low.

If you examine the trajectory table closely, you will see the benefits of a fast-moving arrow. You will also notice that arrow speed alone cannot eliminate the need for accurate range estimation. Another important point to note is how the drop of an arrow compounds as the range increases.

TRAJECTORY TABLE

Initial Arrow Velosity = 180 FPS

Estimated Range In Yards	True Range In Yards	5yd. Miscalculation In Yardage Causes Error in Impact Of:	Estimated Range In Yards	True Range In Yards	5yd. Miscalculation In Yardage Causes Error In Impact Of:
Initial Arrow Velosity = 160 FPS			**Initial Arrow Velosity = 240 FPS**		
20	25	-6.1 INCHES	20	25	-1.9 INCHES
25	30	-8.4 INCHES	25	30	-3.1 INCHES
30	35	-10.6 INCHES	30	35	-4.2 INCHES
35	40	-12.9 INCHES	35	40	-5.2 INCHES
40	45	-15.2 INCHES	40	45	-6.3 INCHES
45	50	-17.6 INCHES	45	50	-7.3 INCHES
50	55	-20.0 INCHES	50	55	-8.3 INCHES
55	60	-22.6 INCHES	55	60	-9.4 INCHES
60	65	-25.3 INCHES	60	65	-10.5 INCHES
Initial Arrow Velosity = 180 FPS			**Initial Arrow Velosity = 260 FPS**		
20	25	-4.5 INCHES	20	25	-1.4 INCHES
25	30	-6.4 INCHES	25	30	-2.5 INCHES
30	35	-8.2 INCHES	30	35	-3.4 INCHES
35	40	-9.9 INCHES	35	40	-4.3 INCHES
40	45	-11.8 INCHES	40	45	-5.2 INCHES
45	50	-13.6 INCHES	45	50	-6.1 INCHES
50	55	-15.5 INCHES	50	55	-7.0 INCHES
55	60	-17.4 INCHES	55	60	-7.9 INCHES
60	65	-19.5 INCHES	60	65	-8.8 INCHES
Initial Arrow Velosity = 200 FPS			**Initial Arrow Velosity = 280 FPS**		
20	25	-3.4 INCHES	20	25	-1.0 INCHES
25	30	-5.0 INCHES	25	30	-1.9 INCHES
30	35	-6.4 INCHES	30	35	-2.8 INCHES
35	40	-7.9 INCHES	35	40	-3.6 INCHES
40	45	-9.3 INCHES	40	45	-4.4 INCHES
45	50	-10.8 INCHES	45	50	-5.2 INCHES
50	55	-12.3 INCHES	50	55	-5.9 INCHES
55	60	-13.9 INCHES	55	60	-6.7 INCHES
60	65	-15.5 INCHES	60	65	-7.5 INCHES
Initial Arrow Velosity = 220 FPS			**Initial Arrow Velosity = 300 FPS**		
20	25	-2.6 INCHES	20	25	-0.7 INCHES
25	30	-3.9 INCHES	25	30	-1.6 INCHES
30	35	-5.2 INCHES	30	35	-2.4 INCHES
35	40	-6.4 INCHES	35	40	-3.1 INCHES
40	45	-7.6 INCHES	40	45	-3.7 INCHES
45	50	-8.8 INCHES	45	50	-4.4 INCHES
50	55	-10.0 INCHES	50	55	-5.1 INCHES
55	60	-11.3 INCHES	55	60	-5.8 INCHES
60	65	-12.6 INCHES	60	65	-6.5 INCHES

RANGE ESTIMATION 3

Bowhunters should understand that range estimation and shooting ability are separate and distinct skills. A tremendous number of excellent shot opportunities are missed because of errors in range estimation. Even after shooting over or under an animal, many bowhunters seem to blame their shooting ability. Range estimation is definitely a weak link in the chain and its importance needs to be fully understood by the bowhunter.

After growing up in the East, my first serious Colorado archery hunt proved to be quite an education. The deer did their best to cooperate, but judging the yardage in the more open terrain was tricky and I always shot low. Long before daylight, about a week into the hunt, I left camp and headed up the mountain armed with a new plan. My new strategy was to add 5 yards to each of my range estimations. Looking back, this was obviously not the best way to solve the problem. But at the time, I was convinced it would work.

It had been light for a while when I stepped

from behind some brush into a clearing. Across a small meadow stood a large bull elk. This was the first bull I had ever seen in the wild, so I doubt that he was as large as he looked. Quickly, I put my new plan into action and added 5 yards to the distance I estimated the bull to be standing. Thinking my problems were solved, I released my arrow. It struck the ground far short and skidded to a stop underneath the bull. He took a step back then indignantly looked down at the arrow and took off for parts unknown. So much for plan "A."

By the end of the trip, I had managed to shoot just over the back of a cow elk. For some reason, this helped my confidence, but more importantly, I understood the significance of range estimation.

After a summer of serious practice, stump shooting and small game hunting, my ability to judge yardage had improved dramatically. The next fall again found me hunting near the meadow where I had missed the bull. My first arrow of the season took a cow elk just behind

the front shoulder. This was a turning point in my bowhunting success.

Shooting in actual hunting terrain at a variety of targets and distances (stump shooting) is the most beneficial form of practice available for the bowhunter who wants to prepare for one-shot hunting opportunities at unknown yardages. Stump shooting should include all types of hunting terrain. If you hunt from treestands, include shooting from them in your practice.

Small game hunting is exciting and, without a doubt, the best form of practice to improve your overall ability as a bowhunter. It will improve your skills in stalking, handling buck fever, shooting ability and range estimation. The best method, however, specifically to im-prove your ability to judge yardage is stump shooting. It gives you the opportunity to take several shots and the chance to verify the distance.

Shooting full-size animal targets can also be

excellent practice (figure 9). When shooting an unmarked range or at full-size animal tar-gets, be aware that you will quickly become familiar with each setting, even if you change shooting positions. All forms of practice are good, but to improve your ability to judge distance, stump shooting offers the most benefit for the least amount of effort.

To help put the importance of accurate range estimation into perspective, I would like to offer the following information. First, for our baseline, I will use a study from the U.S. Army. This study showed that "trained" observers still misjudge distance by an average 17-percent error. With this in mind, we have the following scenario.

Two bowhunters are preparing for the up-coming archery season. Bowhunter Number One is the club champion. He spends all of his spare time at the range, shooting from marked distances, but never spends time in the

Figure 9. Shooting full-size animal targets is excellent practice but targets of this quality take considerable time and effort to construct.

field practicing at unknown distances. He is capable of shooting a 4-inch group at 35 yards. His ability to judge yardage, however, is not good and comes in worse than the army study, at a 24-percent average error. Bowhunter Number Two doesn't get noticed when he shoots at the club, but he has been working hard on his ability to judge yardage. Stump shooting helps his shooting ability, but he is still only a fair shot, capable of shooting a 12-inch group at 35 yards. His ability to judge yardage, however, is excellent, coming in under the U.S. Army study, at a 10-percent error rate.

Now, both bowhunters shoot at a target 35 yards away but they do not know the distance. Both are forced to apply their individual shooting and range-estimating abilities. Although Bowhunter Number One started out as a much better shot, Bowhunter Number Two surpasses him because of his superior ability to judge distance. Bowhunter Number One is now ca-

pable of shooting only a 20-inch group. But bowhunter Number Two is capable of shooting a smaller, 18 inch group.

The reason Bowhunter Number Two surpasses Bowhunter Number One in overall accuracy can be explained by the differences in their ability to judge yardage. Bowhunter Number One misjudged the distance by 24 percent, which is 8.4 yards. We must add 16 inches to Bowhunter Number One's group to allow for the trajectory incurred when there is an 8.4-yard error in range estimation. See figure 10 on next page. Bowhunter Number Two misjudged the distance by 10 percent, which is 3.5 yards. We must add 6 inches to Bowhunter Number Two's group for his error in range estimation.

Again, this gives us a total group size of 20 inches for Bowhunter Number One and a group size of 18 inches for Bowhunter Number Two. If we could combine their abilities, we would

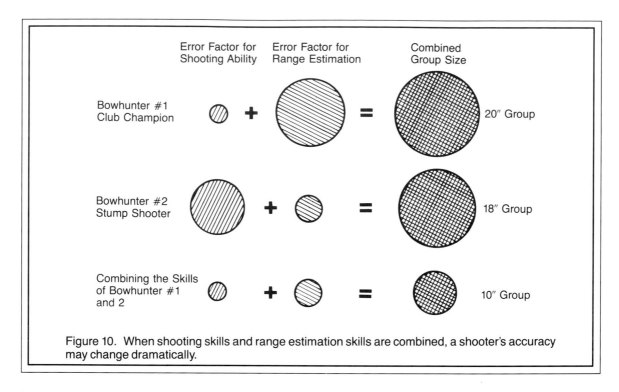

| Error Factor for Shooting Ability | Error Factor for Range Estimation | Combined Group Size |

Figure 10. When shooting skills and range estimation skills are combined, a shooter's accuracy may change dramatically.

have one accurate-shooting bowhunter.

In a real hunting situation, it is unlikely that either bowhunter would make the exact error in range estimation used in our example. Both examples, however, are an average based on each bowhunter's ability to judge distance. Under actual hunting conditions, mistakes in range estimation are often more severe than the 24-percent error made by Bowhunter Number One in our example case.

For those who believe there is no need to worry about range estimation at close distances, the following point may be of interest.

To harvest a deer-sized big game animal cleanly at only 25 yards, you must estimate the distance to your target within 3 to 6 yards, depending on your arrow speed. This information should surprise you. **Many bowhunters' ability to shoot accurately is cancelled out by their inability to judge yardages correctly**.

Range estimation affects freestyle (sights) and bare bow (instinctive) shooters equally. Whether or not there is a sight attached to the bow, the flight path of the arrow will be the same. The only difference is that the sight shooter makes a conscious judgment of the yardage. He then uses a corresponding yardage pin on the bow sight to align with the target before releasing the arrow.

In comparison, the instinctive shooter makes no conscious estimate as to yardage but instead comes to a full draw and releases his arrow when it looks or feels right, like throwing a baseball. You look where you want the arrow to go.

Regardless of the method used, the trajectory paths for both situations are the same if the equipment and shooter are the same. Improving range estimation for instinctive shooters and sight shooters, however, is very different indeed.

INSTINCTIVE SHOOTING

To improve your instinctive shooting ability under actual hunting conditions (those situations where you can expect only one shot in an unfamiliar setting), the following would be helpful. Do as much stump shooting as possible with either your hunting arrows or other arrows with exactly the same flight characteristics. In this case, it would help to have arrows that have the same trajectory and horizontal point of impact as your hunting arrows. This way, it would not be necessary to make any adjustments when changing from practice to hunting arrows.

Standing in the backyard shooting arrow after arrow will help your shooting mechanics but will not do a thing for your ability to estimate distance. To improve your ability to estimate yardage subconsciously, which is what happens when the mind learns to match the trajectory path of the arrow to what your eye sees, you must shoot at unknown distances as often as possible (stump shooting).

Instinctive shooters should be cautious when making equipment changes. Try to shoot the new equipment immediately after any change to make sure the arrow still hits where you think it should. If it does not, you are giving up a portion of what your mind has recorded about matching the trajectory path of your arrow to targets at various distances. If the new equipment has a different point of impact, this information must be relearned.

SIGHT SHOOTING

Sight shooters must sight in to exact yardages to take full advantage of the benefits a sight has to offer. The shooter who does not do this faces many of the same problems plaguing the instinctive shooter. These problems can best be shown by pointing out the advantages of sighting-in at exact yardages.

The bow sighted in to exact yardages allows you to make range estimation a tangible commodity. In other words, 30 yards will always be 30 yards regardless of what else changes. You can change bows, arrows, broadheads—and even anchor points—and what you have learned about judging distances will not be affected. All you need to do is sight in the new equipment to exact yardages and you are right back in business. It also gives you a safety check if your sight pins work loose and move—you can measure out exact yardages and put your sight pins right back to their original location.

The following is a good example of what might happen if you went stump shooting with three friends who didn't have their equipment sighted in to exact yardages.

After shooting at the first target, you ask for opinions on the yardage. Fred says, "It is my third pin." Bill thinks it is 35 paces and Al says, "I don't know, I'm still sighted in for my broadheads and these blunts fly a lot differently." Not only are Fred, Bill and Al doing themselves a disservice, but each shooter, in effect, is speaking a different language and they are not learning much about range estimation.

Sighting in your bow to exact yardages may take a little more effort in the beginning, but it is a standard from which you can learn and a language with which you can communicate with other archers.

Archery equipment, in the hands of an expert shot, can be an extremely accurate rangefinder. The tremendous amount of trajectory or drop in the flight path of the arrow is the reason.

It works like this. You spot a target and estimate the distance to be 25 yards. You shoot an arrow, holding center between your 20- and 30-yard pins (25 yards). When you shoot, the arrow strikes a considerable distance short of the target. You shoot the next arrow, placing your 30 yard pin dead on the target, but the arrow still strikes a little low. With the third arrow, you hold the 30-yard pin just a little high and shoot a "bull's-eye." You take one more shot, again holding your 30-yard pin just a little high, and again shoot a "bull's-eye." If your bow is sighted in to exact yardages with the arrows you are now shooting and you are a very accurate shot, the distance to the above target should be 32 yards, plus or minus a yard.

This type of practice is practical for one-shot hunting opportunities. Because, by learning the correct yardage and how that yardage appears in hunting terrain, your range estimating ability will quickly improve. The more you practice, the more accurate you will become with your first estimate of the distance and your first shot.

The slower the arrow is moving in the above situation, the more accurately the shooter would be able to estimate the distance. This results from the slower arrow dropping more, making any error in range estimation more obvious to the shooter. Remember figure 6 from the trajectory chapter, an arrow moving 180 feet per second (FPS) is dropping almost twice as much for each yard it travels forward as is an arrow moving 240 FPS. The bow that shoots an arrow 180 FPS would be a much more accurate rangefinding device than the bow that shoots an arrow 240 FPS.

For this reason, I like to shoot heavy arrows when stump shooting. This means a slower arrow with more trajectory, which makes my bow and arrow a more accurate rangefinding combination. You could also reduce bow weight, which would cause even more trajectory. Personally, I do not like to reduce my bow weight, preferring to shoot my bow at its hunting weight year round.

Shooting a slower arrow for the purpose of making the bow a more accurate rangefinder is exactly opposite to what should be done

with your hunting equipment. A rotten old stump will allow you several shots before running off; not so a big buck. When hunting, you want as much margin for error as possible on that first shot, hence the need for the flatter shooting bow and arrow combination.

The bow and arrow, when used as a rangefinding device, has no other purpose than that of a tool to help you learn to judge yardage. Even in the hands of a very accurate shot, it is not nearly as accurate as a 100-foot tape. It is, however, a lot more fun and easier to use.

Once, while preparing to measure out a practice range with a friend, I spouted off that I would find the 60-yard mark with my bow and arrows. First, I moved to what my eye said was 60 yards, then shot three arrows, adjusting my distance accordingly each time. I stuck the fourth arrow in the ground for the 60-yard stake. When we measured the distance from the target to my arrow, we found it to be just over 59 yards. It made me feel good, even though it was partly luck. You can make stump shooting a competition in this same manner, rather than shooting for bull's-eyes. This at least makes the drudgery of measuring the distance a little more tolerable.

What about the rangefinders sold specifically for the bowhunter? First, the rangefinder should be accurate in actual hunting terrain to plus or minus 1 yard, nine out of ten times. Some rangefinders are inaccurate and difficult to use. If yours is inaccurate, you may be doing yourself more harm than good. Adjust your rangefinder to scale, from what you feel will be your mid-range shooting distance. For example, if you will be using the rangefinder the most between 20 and 50 yards, set the rangefinder to read accurately at 35 yards. This will help the rangefinder be as accurate as possible at your primary distances.

After the rangefinder is adjusted, test it on an accurately measured course. If it passes this test, move on to a variety of hunting terrains, lighting conditions and target outlines. Check the rangefinder under these conditions with an accurate measuring device, such as a 100-foot tape, for the plus or minus 1 yard error. If the rangefinder passes this test, you should feel comfortable using it as a learning tool while stump shooting and while hunting if so desired.

If you plan to use a rangefinder while hunting, the only consideration in regard to accuracy is that it should surpass *your* ability to judge yardage. If you do carry a rangefinder while hunting, it is highly unlikely that you will have time to use it in all situations. With this in mind, it is best to learn to judge distance quickly and accurately without using the rangefinder. Personally, I prefer using a rangefinder only as a learning tool while stump shooting.

STUMP SHOOTING (FOR THE SIGHT SHOOTER)

The most common and enjoyable way to improve range estimation is to stump shoot. This is done by roaming typical hunting terrain and picking anything that stands out as a target and attempting a shot. Stump shooting can be combined with scouting if it is the time of year that the disturbance would not affect your hunting area. When stump shooting:

- Always keep safety in mind.
- Blunts work best for stump shooting (figure 11). I prefer HTM rubber blunts. They help protect the arrow by absorbing some of the shock and do not go underground easily. Judo points also work very well.
- Unless you plan to buy stock in an arrow company, choose only targets that are somewhat soft.

To get the most from stump shooting you will need the following:

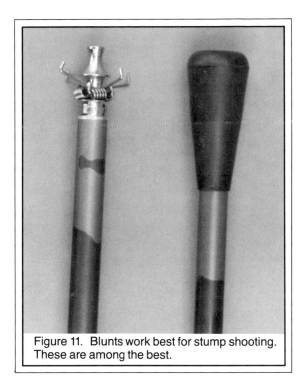

Figure 11. Blunts work best for stump shooting. These are among the best.

- A bow and arrow combination sighted in to the exact yardages with blunt-equipped arrows.
- A good measuring device—both a 100-foot tape and light rope without much stretch work well. If you use rope, it should be marked at every yard after 20 yards. It is helpful to use different color markings to distinguish the one-, five- and ten-yard numbers on the rope.
- One or more friends—this makes measuring the distance a lot less work.
- Rangefinder—optional. This is an excellent opportunity to learn to use the rangefinder and check its ability to give accurate readings under actual hunting conditions.

Once the above have been accomplished, the only thing left is to locate a good place to shoot. Try to select a location that is similar to hunting terrain. Some hunters are fortunate enough to have a good place to stump shoot near home. For most of us, it is not that easy. Once you find a good location, I suggest the following:

When one person spots a target (hopefully soft), he points it out to the others. Yardage is not discussed and the spotter shoots first. Then, take turns shooting until each person feels he can make an accurate estimation of the yardage (figure 12A). Only then does each shooter voice his opinion as to yardage. As your ability improves, the number of arrows you need to hit the target will be reduced. If you have a rangefinder, use it before moving but after your shooting is completed and note that estimate also.

Now use your measuring device and use it accurately. To do this, one person stays at the shooting position, the other moves to the target (figure 12B). If you misjudged the yardage by more than plus or minus 1 yard, move back to the shooting position and, while looking at the target, tell yourself the distance you now know is correct. Also shoot at the target one more time, using the correct yardage.

When your shooting ability or the rangefinder's ability allows you to estimate the distance within plus or minus 1 yard nine out of ten times, you would be safe in doing away with the measuring device.

To maximize your learning potential from stump shooting, you must know the exact yardage. If you just say to yourself, "I think that stump is 35 yards away," and do not use a positive method of finding out whether or not you were correct, chances are you have done more harm than good. Finding the exact yardage each time is tedious work and not much fun, but the correct answer is a vital step toward improving your ability to estimate distance. Learning to judge yardage accurately will help you eliminate many missed shots.

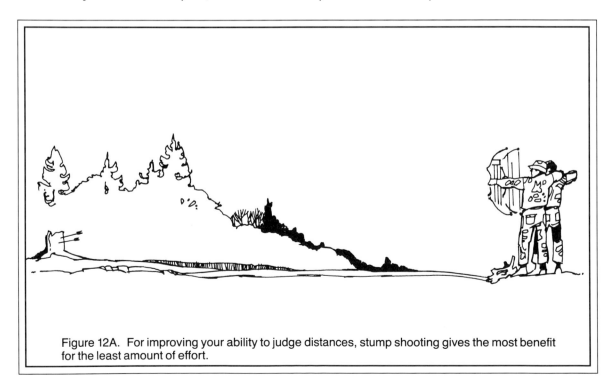

Figure 12A. For improving your ability to judge distances, stump shooting gives the most benefit for the least amount of effort.

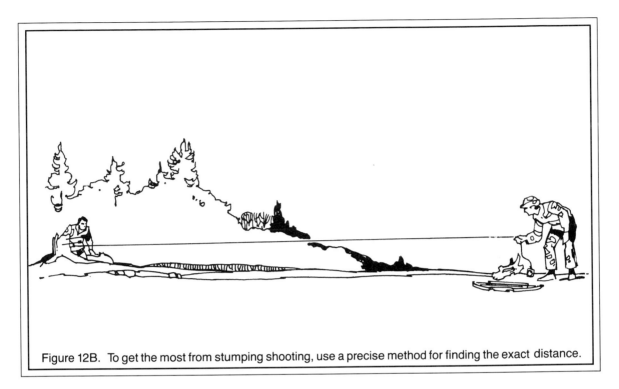

Figure 12B. To get the most from stumping shooting, use a precise method for finding the exact distance.

Many bowhunters trust their pacing ability 100 percent. Some are very good on flat level ground. But if they are forced to pace the distance through downed timber, gulches, etc., chances are that much of the accuracy is lost. The point here is to make very sure the answer is correct, regardless of the method used to find that answer.

As stated before, the bow and arrow combination can be an accurate rangefinder. In fact, it is one of the most accurate available today for the price. Consider the fact that most of us already have these items and this is a good deal. The only factor that limits the accuracy of the bow and arrow as a rangefinder is the shooting ability of the person behind the bow.

My most effective method for judging distance is to pay close attention to the amount of detail I am able see in the target or animal. See figure 13 on the next page. Each person's visual abilities are slightly different, so this method must be adapted individually through trial and error. You should practice this while stump shooting. Look for minute changes in the detail of the target. Do the same while hunting; look at the head, eyes, ears, hair, etc. Many hunters try to judge yardage by the size of the animal. This can cause problems because critters come in all sizes. Looking for detail when judging yardage helps eliminate the size problem and has been very effective for me. Another plus is that there is no need to take my eyes off the animal.

If you use this method be aware that you will need to make adjustments for weather and light conditions. For instance, I have a tendency to overjudge the yardage during conditions such as poor light, haze, drizzle and fog. I am inclined to underjudge yardage in bright sunlight, open areas and on snow-covered ground.

There are no set rules for estimating distance.

Figure 13. The visual loss of detail is subtle as the range increases. Learn to see that change if you plan to use this method of judging distance.

Use the method that works best for you. The most important aspect is to practice judging yardage on a regular basis or you will lose the ability very quickly.

The advantage to sighting in to exact yardages is that each sight pin is set for the same distance year after year. In other words, you do not lose what you have learned about range estimation from experience just because you changed a piece of equipment or your sight pins have worked loose and moved.

This is also true when learning to judge yardage. Basically, this is how it works. If you look at enough objects and estimate the distance to those objects in hunting terrain (stump shooting), your mind will quickly learn from both the correct and incorrect estimates. The trick is to verify the yardage with a measuring device so you will positively know when you were correct and when you were not. It should also be kept in mind that 10 one-hour practice sessions are much better than one 10-hour practice session. Spaced repetition is the key. Judging yardage must be practiced on a regular basis to maintain a high level of accuracy.

If your hunting situations require you to shoot at unknown distances, please be aware of the need for accurate range estimation. Stump shooting, in the manner described in this chapter, is a very beneficial form of practice and it's fun!

BUCK FEVER 4

You may have heard the story about the young fellow out west on his first guided hunt. Upon seeing a huge bull elk, he promptly levered all the cartridges from his rifle while yelling "bang" each time. The hunter could not be convinced that he had missed the bull until the guide showed him the unfired cartridges on the ground.

Here is another buck fever story, related to me by G. Fred Asbell, President of the Pope and Young club. Fred and another fellow were hunting bighorn sheep in the Colorado mountains. Fred was in the lead when a herd of rams was suddenly spotted at close range. Fred's companion rushed past Fred, knocking him to the ground. Once in front, he proceeded to shoot an arrow several yards over the back of a ram standing 15 yards away. He then systematically removed three more arrows from his quiver and dropped them on the ground. His final arrow was shot high in the air as the last ram made its way to parts unknown. When the action was over, this hunter could not be convinced that he had knocked Fred to the ground or that the arrows had not fallen from a "faulty quiver."

Both stories involved severe cases of buck fever. These examples probably fit the mold most hunters imagine when they think of buck fever. Well, there is a lot more to buck fever— and a lot less. Fortunately, most of us don't suffer as severely as these hunters.

It is natural to become excited when you spot a big game animal and believe you are about to get a shot. It happens to everyone. Just getting excited, however, is not buck fever. There is a fine line between the excitement of hunting and buck fever. That line is crossed when we make mistakes solely because of the excitement or pressure. These mistakes are not limited to shooting errors, as many assume. Buck fever can include shooting or moving at the wrong time, errors in range estimation, hitting unseen tree limbs, making unnecessary noise, etc.

How do you tell the difference between a

coincidental oversight and an error made primarily because of buck fever? With the small mistakes, it's really difficult to tell and only you can be the judge. But a good clue is when and how consistently these foul-ups occur. Another test I have found that correlates very well to buck fever is the memory. The more a hunter suffers from buck fever, the less he seems to remember about the encounter with the animal. At least, he recalls less about the small details and what really happened.

For the purpose of this discussion, **buck fever** is defined as becoming so excited and/ or wanting to succeed to such a high degree that mentally and physically you fail to perform to your full potential. You function at a level substantially below your normal standard, especially in regard to shooting ability. As the size of the trophy or the importance of the shot increases, so does the potential for buck fever.

Buck fever includes snap shooting, freezing above or below the target, not aiming or concentrating on the kill zone (not picking a spot), etc. If any of these situations occur while shooting targets, it is called **target panic**. When this occurs while hunting, it is referred to as buck fever. These terms are interchangeable because the root cause is the same; be it panic or fever, **the trouble starts in your head**. The end result is that the shooter does not have full control over how the arrow is shot. As stated in the definition, you want to succeed so much that the opposite result actually occurs.

While it is true that most of us don't start shaking when we see a paper target on a hay bale like we sometimes do when we spot a real critter, the reason for missing both is often the same. The difference is only a matter of degree. Buck fever and target panic are very real. To overcome or guard against this strange affliction, you need to understand the problem. Many times, during discussions regarding this subject, I have heard fellows known for their severe bouts of buck fever say something like this: "If I didn't get excited, I wouldn't hunt." That's just an attempt to rationalize the problem. We all get excited or we wouldn't hunt.

You might compare buck fever to a medicine. The right amount can be very beneficial; too much can be damaging, even fatal. If the truth were known, in hunting accidents where misidentification of the target is involved (human for animal), I believe most—if not all—cases involve a high degree of buck fever. A person must be extremely excited to make such a terrible mistake. As tragic as these cases are, fortunately, they are quite rare considering the number of hunters afield.

Most of us suffer from buck fever to some degree and many times it is just enough to cause us to miss an important shot. But thankfully, the buck fever most of us suffer is not severe enough to cause a tragic mental error such as mistaking a hunter for an animal. If the following scenario could be run in real life with 100 different hunters, I believe it would consistently turn out like this:

Joe is in his treestand, before dawn, opening morning of the archery season. Last year he shot his first deer, a doe, late in the season. Joe has told himself, his wife and friends that this year he is going to hunt bucks only for the first week of the season. Now it's late in the morning, Joe hasn't seen a thing and he is beginning to remember just how difficult it had been last year. Just as Joe is ready to give up for the day, he sees a doe approaching. He is torn between what he has told his wife and friends and the possibility of getting a shot. The doe stops broadside at Joe's maximum effective shooting range. As Joe draws his bow, there is no pressure to succeed. He thinks, "I'll probably miss anyway and if I do, I won't have to explain why I changed my mind." Joe releases!

Most likely, Joe has an 80- to 90-percent chance of harvesting the doe because there is little or no buck fever involved. But if we change that doe to a huge Pope and Young buck, his chances for success would drop to 10 percent or less. At the sight of a monster buck, Joe, in all likelihood, would contract a severe case of the shakes. Unfortunately, that is the way buck fever works; the more important the shot becomes, the less likely we are to function at a 100 percent level of effectiveness.

As a general rule, buck fever affects the bowhunter more severely than it does the rifle hunter. There are several reasons for this: (a) bowhunters are under the physical strain of holding the draw weight of the bow; (b) the bow is a more difficult weapon to use in hunting situations and the bowhunter knows he must function at 100 percent; (c) the bowhunter must approach much closer to his quarry, thus adding to the pressure and excitement.

Buck fever is mental in origin but affects the way we function physically. Everyone is susceptible to the pressures of buck fever. Some hunters have the ability to control their excitement to a point that it has little or no effect on their ability to shoot accurately or react correctly. Experience and mental attitude play a major role in mastering this sometimes elusive ability.

The following experience illustrates how a hunting partner can help control buck fever. Late one fall afternoon, a friend and I were glassing a distant ridge for mule deer. That summer I had been helping Tom with his fight against buck fever. All of a sudden, he whispered, "Here comes a buck!" Tom only had time to grab his bow and slap an arrow on the string before the fork-horn buck caught movement and stopped broadside 25 yards away. Tom shot a rushed arrow that missed the buck. The forky only moved a few yards then turned broadside once again. Tom also rushed his second shot and missed. This time, the buck moved to a little beyond 30 yards and turned broadside for one last look. As Tom came to full draw, I whispered, "Take your time!" as I had said to him many times that summer on the practice range. Tom aimed for several seconds, then shot a perfect arrow, striking the forky right behind the shoulder. Later, as we dressed the deer, Tom told me that my talking to him had helped. That buck was the turning point for Tom and he has managed to control buck fever ever since.

Many times, the calm voice of a friend or guide can reduce buck fever. Unfortunately, you never know what the animal's reaction to your voice will be, particularly with bowhunting where the shooting distances are so close. Sometimes, it's surprising what an animal will tolerate, especially if you just whisper. But, I never try this method unless the hunter has

already missed a shot. If you are alone and start to get nervous, silently talk to yourself; you might be amazed how much it will help. Several little tricks can help you control buck fever. Staying calm is a very important one.

For several years, I had the opportunity to observe as two ladies became involved in hunting. They had no previous experience and both started hunting at the suggestion of their husbands. Ultimately, the same pattern emerged. Both were as cool as cucumbers and very accurate shots for the first few years. As their love for hunting and their desire to succeed developed, they became susceptible to buck fever and their shooting ability was affected. As their experience grew and their confidence returned, so did their shooting ability.

Experience and confidence are two extremely important elements in dealing with buck fever. The amount that they help in controlling the problem varies significantly from

individual to individual. For the majority of hunters, however, the benefits gained from both experience and confidence are indisputable.

If you are just starting your bowhunting career, try not to let your tag go unfilled waiting for "Mister Big." Harvesting that first big game animal is an important step in building both confidence and experience. Any game animal taken legally with archery equipment is a trophy of which a bowhunter should be proud. There will be plenty of time to set your goals a little higher.

The animals you attempt to harvest should be determined by the game regulations and your own personal choice, not by "the boys at the bar." In many cases, it is a sound game management practice to harvest a doe, spike buck or even a fawn. Check with your state game department. Ask to speak to a biologist familiar with the herd structure in your hunting area. Also contact your local conservation officer for his opinion on the effects of harvesting females and young animals from the herd in your hunting area.

Small game hunting can pay big dividends in helping a bowhunter reduce the effects of buck fever. Buck fever might be compared to being bitten by a rattlesnake. If the first time doesn't kill you, the next bite won't be so bad, and so on, until you build up your immunity. Small game hunting will give you buck fever in smaller doses and will help you become more familiar with shooting at animals. It's also helpful in all other aspects of bowhunting, from stalking, to shooting, to range estimation. The overall benefits associated with small game hunting cannot be overemphasized.

Scouting, observing and being close to animals is helpful in reducing the effects of buck fever. Even observing animals at the zoo or on a farm helps you get to know them and feel more comfortable in their presence. Tree-stands offer the unique opportunity to observe animals, at close range in their natural habitat and help you learn to anticipate their movements and reactions. Photography is another possibility. For good pictures, you must get very close to the animal, and in this way, the experience is very similar to bowhunting.

Many years ago, while bowhunting in Pennsylvania, I came upon a huge whitetail buck at 15 yards as I rounded a large pine tree. Because of a severe case of buck fever, I came to half draw and released. At first, it upset me that I had missed such a trophy. But after thinking about the situation, it became clear that even if I had harvested the animal, I would not have been proud of myself because of the way I shot the arrow. In addition, because of my buck fever, there was a tremendous chance of only wounding that buck.

From that day on, I made myself a promise to shoot every arrow at game to the best of my ability. Then, if the shot was missed because I misjudged the yardage or for some other reason, I could still feel good about my effort. The secret for me has been to make it **more important to shoot the arrow correctly than to harvest the animal**. It didn't take long to realize that when the arrow was shot correctly, my accuracy automatically improved.

Believe me, it was not easy. In the beginning, I missed shots because of the fight going on internally. Half of me wanted to rush the shot, the other half wanted to shoot the arrow correctly. The mistakes I had a tendency to make at the time of the shot had to be fought every step of the way. Each time I succeeded, however, the fight became a little easier and soon my buck fever was under control. Today, when shooting at an animal I devote my total concentration to shooting the arrow like I have a thousand times before in practice. The trick is not to do anything different or fancy but just to complete the shot with normal shooting form.

When I succeed at this seemingly simple task and have judged the yardage correctly, the shot is usually a good one—yours will be too.

CONQUERING BUCK FEVER

The holding weight of the bow is believed to be a contributing cause of buck fever and target panic. I feel this is particularly true for heavy recurve and long bow shooters. But with today's compounds, most shooters are not holding a great deal of weight. While reducing the holding weight of the bow will help in some cases, I don't feel this action alone will totally cure buck fever for many bowhunters.

There are other methods and devices that can help you control buck fever. Trying something new is always difficult, but so are the disadvantages of buck fever. The next few pages will summarize four approaches that can help you overcome buck fever. Whatever meth-ods you use, remember, the first step is to admit to yourself and others that you have the problem. Experiencing buck fever is very common and there is no reason to be ashamed. Close observation has taught me that over 95 percent of all bowhunters experience some degree of buck fever or target panic during their careers and most are unsuccessful at totally eliminating the problem. If this number is surprising, it is because many bowhunters work hard at hiding their problem. By controlling buck fever and target panic, you will enjoy shooting the bow more than you ever thought possible.

There is one very important point about trying something new to overcome buck fever. It is essential to make the new method work on the very first arrow and for several arrows thereafter until you are confident it will help you. Try to set your mind to this point before starting.

It is helpful to stand very close (five yards or so) to a large backstop. This helps most people relax. Do not place a target on the backstop. Concentrate on making the new method work (shooting the arrow correctly), not on hitting a spot or even shooting a group. It may be helpful to close your eyes the first few times and just think about shooting the arrow. If this method is employed, for safety reasons, move to within a few feet of the backstop and make sure you have an observer.

A point to keep in mind when shooting at very close range is that the arrows may bend when striking the backstop or target. This is most likely to occur when shooting a heavy bow at a firm backstop. To avoid this problem, use a lighter bow, (which is a good idea anyway), old or heavy arrows and a soft backstop.

It is best to begin with a very light draw-weight bow to reduce muscle tension when trying a new method of shooting. As mentioned, begin at close range and shoot until you are convinced that the new technique will help you. Then put up a target and increase the distance slowly. Early on, if you fail to shoot even one arrow without proper mental control, start over with the close-range practice.

To realize the maximum benefit from any change in shooting style, you must begin with a positive frame of mind and make an honest effort to succeed. Here are the strongest methods you can use in your effort to gain control over buck fever:

COUNTING

The rules for this method are as follows: You must reach full draw and count to two before releasing. You cannot start counting until you are at full draw, anchored and holding where you want the arrow to go. If you try this method, make sure you never release before you silently finish saying the word "two."

This method offers only minimal additional control. The secret is to make sure you make it work every time. Be prepared to fight the urge to release before you finish counting.

Counting is also recommended for the individual who experiences very little buck fever but would like a little extra control for those very important shots. If you plan to use this method while hunting, practice it ahead of time.

MECHANICAL RELEASE

First, you must be willing to try a release. If using a release is unacceptable to you, go on to the next suggestion. Another possible drawback to the release is that it works much better in conjunction with a sight because of the low anchor point necessary for most people to shoot a release properly. I am sure a determined, instinctive shooter could become very accurate using a release, but it might be difficult.

If you decide to try a release, be patient. Give yourself plenty of time to become familiar with the different feel. More than likely, the transition won't come easy, but release aids can work wonders for certain people. One summer, I assisted a friend who was on the verge of giving up bowhunting after 11 years because of buck fever and inaccurate shooting. A release helped him overcome buck fever and improved his shooting ability. Now, three years later, he is an excellent shot and is enjoying bowhunting to its fullest. That's what it's all about.

A release will generally improve a bowhunter's shooting ability in addition to helping with buck fever. If you are interested in trying a release, read the section on release aids in the "Accessories" chapter. Again, if you are using a release to assist with buck fever or target panic, make sure you start with a light draw weight bow and shoot with the proper mental control from the very first arrow.

THE CLICKER

The clicker is a device that signals the shooter when to release by a small, audible sound, which gives the clicker its name. The clicking sound is usually created by flexing a small piece of spring steel. A variety of clicker designs incorporate this principle. A device is also available which visibly signals the shooter when to shoot (the broadhead timer). Both of these devices are triggered by the shooter as he increases his draw length while aiming. The shooter releases the arrow immediately upon the audible or visible signal.

For those not familiar with clickers, allow me to make a few comments. First, if you have any doubt about the effectiveness of the clicker, check the archers competing at the Olympic level. Most, if not all, of these shooters use a clicker (figure 14). Of course, the type of clicker used for target equipment and hunting tackle will vary considerably.

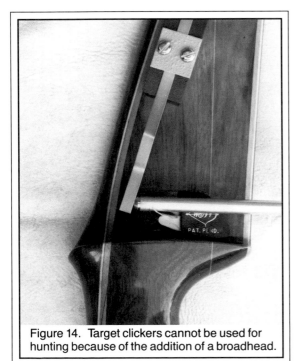

Figure 14. Target clickers cannot be used for hunting because of the addition of a broadhead.

Clickers were developed for use by target shooters. The arrow, equipped with a target point, is placed beneath a small arm made from spring steel which is placed in a location precisely to match the shooter's draw length. When the arrow is drawn back beyond the clicker, the spring steel arm slaps against the bow, emitting a small click which signals the shooter to release the arrow.

This device works very well for target shooters in controlling target panic, and it is very effective for bowhunters who are willing to use one. The type of clickers used by target shooters could not be adapted to hunting due to the addition of a broadhead to the arrow. Other variations of the clicker were developed specifically for the bowhunter. We will discuss these in detail later.

The reasons the clicker-type devices work so well to help control target panic and buck fever are:

- They give you a signal when to shoot and you can train yourself to wait for this signal.
- They give you a task to perform while aiming.
- They give you the exact same draw length for each shot.
- While aiming, you must draw the bow another ⅛ inch. This gives you good back tension and a better release.

There are clickers available for hunting bows and they do work. One model attaches to the upper limb and to the bow string. This model will work either on a compound or recurve bow. See figure 15 on the next page. It is offered by Clickery Klick Products (5001 N. Dawn Drive, Peoria, IL 61614). The sound of the Clickery Klick model can be reduced by adding a little tape to the spring steel portion of the clicker. Other clicker designs and brands are also available.

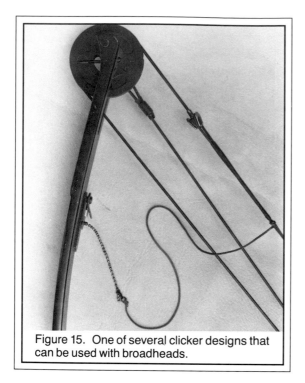

Figure 15. One of several clicker designs that can be used with broadheads.

or so of the draw. Most broadhead timers will work equally well on both compound and recurve bows. One quality broadhead timer currently on the market is the Frydenlund Timer, offered by the Motor Miter Co. (P.O. Box 37, Prairie du Chien, WI 53821).

The broadhead timer offers the greatest amount of control because it actually rides over the arrow shaft (figure 16). If the arrow is released before the timer is triggered, there will be damage to the arrow fletching and the timer itself. For some reason, this knowledge seems to control even severe cases of (snap-shooting) buck fever.

The degree of buck fever you experience will dictate which of the above methods you may want to try. They offer an increasing amount of control in the order listed. Again, if you decide to try something new, you should make it work on the very first arrow. You must convince yourself to shoot the arrow right;

The first question, and a natural one, is about the noise the clicker makes just as the shooter releases. I know one bowhunter who has harvested several big game animals using a clicker. He reports that he has not experienced any problems with animals jumping the string. But with any extra noise, the possibility exists that there could be a problem from time to time.

BROADHEAD TIMER

Another device similar to the clicker is called the broadhead timer. The difference with the broadhead timer is that it signals the hunter visually when to release rather than with a sound.

The broadhead timer works by signaling the shooter with a small metal arm that flips up. This spring-type arm is dislodged by the broad-head as the shooter completes the last ⅛ inch

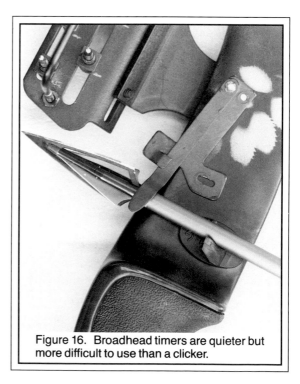

Figure 16. Broadhead timers are quieter but more difficult to use than a clicker.

nothing else matters. If you shoot the arrow correctly, the accuracy will come. I'm not trying to tell you it will be easy. But it can be done and that's what's important.

Broadhead timers and clickers have been around for a long time, but they never did become extremely popular with the general bowhunting public. This may be because their benefits are not fully understood. Another reason could be that most of us don't believe that we should have to add a silly little device to our bows to fight something we can't even see. Whatever the reasons, untold numbers of bowhunters go through years of frustration unnecessarily.

When compared to the disadvantages of severe buck fever, such as not being able to reach anchor before releasing, not being able to aim where you want, and other problems, the inconvenience of a clicker or broadhead timer is a small price to pay.

Many bowhunters turn to snap shooting in an effort to control buck fever, but this usually affects accuracy considerably. If you are a bowhunter who suffers severe accuracy problems because of buck fever or target panic, at least consider trying a clicker or broadhead timer.

Most bowhunters are familiar with the term "pick a spot." This generally means to pick a small spot on the animal to shoot at rather than shooting at the entire animal. Many bowhunters even write this phrase on their bows to help them remember it in hunting situations. We have all heard these words used as advice but also as an excuse for missing. As advice, it is sound, but as an excuse it doesn't hold water. If a bowhunter tells himself to "pick a spot" over and over while practicing, then forgets to

do so on those few shots at animals, the true reason for forgetting such a critical part of the shot is buck fever.

Two important points are hidden in the "pick a spot" message. (1) To avoid facing the buck fever problem, we sometimes incorrectly place the blame: "I didn't pick a spot." (2) The true message from this phrase is very important and that is to stay calm. If you do, you'll remember to "pick a spot."

Experience and confidence have been addressed and their importance cannot be overstated. These tools, by themselves, can sometimes overcome buck fever. Whatever method you use to combat buck fever, experience and confidence will help.

The bowhunter who waits five years for a monster buck and then takes his first shot has a high probability of missing. Choices such as these are personal ones, as they should be, but remember, positive experiences build confidence. The confidence you can gain by harvesting a few animals is a big step in the fight against buck fever. Knowing you can do it is a very important step. Thinking you may not, is disaster.

Buck fever varies so much from individual to individual that it must be addressed on a personal level. From experience, I am very familiar with target panic during competition and severe buck fever while hunting. Buck fever has not affected my shooting accuracy for many years thanks to some of the methods listed in this chapter. With determination and the right frame of mind, they can do the same for you. If you suffer from buck fever, fight back. The battle can be won!

BALANCING YOUR SKILLS 5

Bowhunting big game animals is a difficult challenge, even for the most experienced hunters. If you put in the time and effort, however, the shot opportunities will come. How you handle those opportunities is the bottom line. To be at your very best, you should begin preparing long before the season opens.

Few of us have all the time we need to prepare properly for the upcoming season. How we spend the time we do have is critical. Even though you may not have the time necessary to become 100 percent efficient in all areas covered in this book, it is best to even out or balance your abilities. The point is not to leave huge holes in your offensive line. This chapter summarizes how the skills discussed on the preceding pages fit into the overall bowhunting picture. The idea is to evaluate your skills and hunting methods, then spend your practice time in the most productive and enjoyable way possible.

When opening day arrives, your effectiveness as a bowhunter is only as good as the weakest

link in the chain to success. In many cases, a bowhunter's ability to shoot accurately in a hunting situation is as dependent on range estimating skill, arrow trajectory and the capability to overcome buck fever, as on shooting ability. Regardless of experience level, it's every bowhunter's responsibility to strive toward improving and strengthening his or her abilities in these areas.

You can eliminate the range estimation and trajectory sections if you shoot at 20 yards and under or only at known distances. Limiting your shots to a distance that matches your shooting skill is always an excellent idea. To do that, however, you must be able to estimate yardage accurately out to the distance you have set as your maximum effective range. Estimating the distance to animals and using rangefinders in hunting situations may both be more difficult than you realize. In talking with bowhunters, I find that many underestimate the importance of range estimation and trajectory, particularly between 20 and 30 yards.

As mentioned earlier, I harvested six Pope and Young animals and a coyote with seven shots in the same season. The major reason for my success is that I always work hard to improve and balance all areas covered in this chapter. In the introduction to this book, I also mentioned reaching the summit of my bowhunting career. Well that certainly was a summit, but it isn't meant to imply that I don't continue to learn and improve. The bowhunter who believes he knows everything there is to know about animals, archery equipment or his own abilities is very foolish indeed.

Learning to bowhunt might be compared to putting together a picture puzzle with both very large and very small pieces. The large pieces go together quickly at first but then progress slows. At times, you become frustrated. Then one day, you recognize a beautiful picture taking shape before you. After savoring your success, you realize there are still many small pieces necessary to complete the puzzle. Bowhunting fits that mold because it provides enjoyment and occasional success to the beginner while providing that same enjoyment plus a continual challenge to even the most experienced hunter.

SHOOTING ABILITY

Shooting ability is a cornerstone in the foundation of any bowhunter's success. We must all learn to shoot at a reasonably accurate level before attempting to bowhunt. To beat the odds by luck alone is not much of an accomplishment. There will, however, always be a few who try to sneak by without paying their dues. It is particularly distressful to me when someone like this is successful, as in this story.

Some time ago, I was assisting a friend at his elk camp. One of his hunters was a terrible shot. He was lucky to hit a 24-inch target from 20 yards away but fully expected to harvest an

elk. This fellow—I refuse to call him a hunter—harvested the largest bull of the season at my friend's camp. He missed the bull at 10 yards and then made a clean shot at 45 yards. To top things off, he sat in camp the rest of the week and never shot another arrow. He honestly believed he was an excellent bowhunter; after all, he had a big bull elk as proof.

If you depend totally on luck, as this fellow did, in most cases, you will be bitterly disappointed. There must be a balance of many skills before anyone can become a consistently successful bowhunter.

Regardless of its importance, we all should realize that shooting ability will not, by itself, ensure success. Many bowhunters spend the majority of their spare time and effort trying to improve their target shooting skills. This is easy to understand because many of us live in or near large towns and it is much more convenient to shoot in the back yard or drive to a nearby range.

There is nothing wrong with target practice and it's gratifying to see improvements on a paper target. Archery should be fun and we must practice our shooting skills often. Unfortunately, many of us succumb to a target-practice-only routine and are consequently out of balance. In addition to target practice, you should allow time to improve the other skills necessary to become a consistently successful bowhunter. Learn to identify, then concentrate on improving the areas of weakness in your skills.

RANGE ESTIMATION

Range estimation, in reality, is no more important than shooting ability, trajectory or the effects of buck fever, but experience has shown me this is the one area which bowhunters neglect. Many bowhunters fail to understand the importance of, and need for, accurate range estimation. Consequently, most of us fail to give this area the practice necessary. Significant improvement can be made with the proper practice.

After bowhunting, guiding and assisting friends for many years, I cannot tell you how many arrows I have watched fly just over or under some very respectable big game animals. In many of these cases, the only error made was that of range estimation. This is sad, considering all the time, effort and luck that goes into getting a shot at a quality big game animal.

Do not misunderstand me; everyone is going to blow stalks and miss shots. That's bowhunting. But the closer you get to success the more it hurts to fail. Then to find that you could have made a good stab at curing the problem beforehand makes the situation even more disappointing. Most bowhunters could make significant improvement in their ability to judge yardage with a little serious practice.

BUCK FEVER

This is the "between" from between a rock and a hard place. If you have ever experienced buck fever, you know all too well what I'm talking about. The cause of buck fever is 100 percent mental. It certainly becomes physical and I have seen hunters completely unable to draw the bow. Still, the root of the poisonous tree begins in the mind. You are the only one who honestly knows how much buck fever affects you.

You should have an idea of how buck fever might affect you even if you have never released an arrow at a big game animal. Were your knees shaking when you thought you might get a shot? How about at the range, shooting against your buddies, when your last arrow decided the winner? Even alone in the backyard, shooting the last arrow in your best ever group. How about when your sight pin will not stop on the bull's-eye?

Yes, buck fever is an all too real problem. The best way to win the battle is to meet the problem head on. To do that, you must first admit to yourself that you are susceptible to buck fever. Only then can you work toward improving the situation. Don't think you are alone. Most of us have been there and many of us still are. I'm not sure anyone ever cures buck fever—I think we just learn to control the problem.

The way I learned to control my own buck fever was to make it more important to shoot the arrow correctly than it was to fill my tag. The best way to explain this situation is with a short story.

Larry spots a new world record Pope and Young bull elk. He calls in the bull and has the opportunity for a 30-yard broadside shot. Now Larry gets to choose which shot he wants to live with:

A. Larry gets a severe case of buck fever. He

jerks his bow to half-draw and shoots the arrow toward the ground. The arrow hits a log and glances into the bull's heart with just enough penetration to do the job. The bull travels 100 yards and collapses.

B. Larry is naturally excited, his heart is racing 100 miles per hour, but somehow he reaches deep inside. He comes to full draw, anchors, then holds on a spot just behind the bull's front shoulder and releases smoothly. At that very instant, a falling pine cone deflects Larry's arrow and he misses the bull.

The day Larry honestly chooses shot B, he will never succumb to buck fever again. Few of us would pass that test, including this writer. The problem is that it is more important to us to harvest an animal than it is to shoot the arrow correctly. This is a weakness buck fever thrives on; it is a mind game that many bow-hunters lose.

TRAJECTORY

Arrow trajectory is obviously very important but it is more a function of decision than it is practice. You may want to add just a few pounds of draw weight, go all out to obtain as much arrow speed as possible, or do nothing at all. The choice is a personal one.

Here is a story that subtly shows how the four skills discussed in this chapter can each affect the outcome of a hunt.

It was a cold evening and snow was starting to fall as I left the treestand I had placed early that same afternoon. Even though I had seen only one deer that first evening, I was confident the treestand was in the right location. Hoping for snow by morning, I headed for camp. I'm not sure fresh snow is important when hunting whitetail deer from treestands during the rut, but personally, I enjoy hunting on a fresh snow more than anything in the world. Early the next morning, I was ecstatic to find four inches

of soft, fluffy snow lying under a moonless sky full of bright stars.

In my excitement to get an early start, I unknowingly put the wrong box of arrows in my truck. This mistake wasn't apparent until I parked the truck and was ready to head for my stand. By then it was too late to return to camp for more arrows. Fortunately, there were two broadhead-equipped arrows mixed with my blunts in the arrow box. Heading off into the darkness, I thought, "I'm not going to be late even if it means going to the stand with no arrows at all."

As I walked along, I could not remember ever getting more than one shot a day when hunting trophy whitetail bucks. I always carry several broadheads, however, just so I am never faced with a wounded animal and no arrows. This was my only real reason for concern with having only two arrows.

But the arrow situation was temporarily forgotten as I started to climb to my stand and noticed a deer track in the fresh snow only a few yards from the tree. Not long after sunrise, a small buck and three does passed by at less than 20 yards without becoming aware of my presence. When deer pass by within easy bow range, without becoming suspicious, it builds my confidence immensely.

After the deer were out of sight, nothing stirred for quite a while and my thoughts drifted back to my arrow situation. I was not satisfied with the sharpness of the second arrow when I'd checked it earlier at the truck. Wanting to make sure it was razor sharp, I removed the blades from the head and proceeded to touch them up with a small steel.

About halfway through the sharpening process, I spotted a coyote hunting its way in my direction. Many bowhunters have told me about the coyotes and foxes they have passed up because they didn't want to take a chance on spooking a deer. Personally, I believe a coyote or fox is a much more unusual trophy to harvest than a deer. To each his own, but I wasn't about to let this one walk by even if I did have only two arrows.

When the coyote reached approximately 40 yards, it was evident that his direction of travel wouldn't bring him any closer. I drew and placed the 40 yard pin a few feet in front of his nose because he was moving at a fast walk. Just after releasing, I was amazed to see the arrow make a solid hit. The coyote turned and tried to run but only traveled 30 yards before collapsing in the snow. I was excited and wanted to climb down and collect my coyote, but it was still early and I could see the coyote wasn't going anywhere. So, I decided to stay in my treestand for a few more hours.

Not 10 minutes later, just after I finished sharpening my remaining arrow, a doe crossed a small opening headed in my direction. Because I was reaching for my bow, I only caught a glimpse of a second deer about 30 yards behind her. Both deer continued in my direction and even through the brush, I could tell the second deer was a nice buck. The doe turned slightly, which meant she was going to pass on the downwind side of my stand. About 30 yards downwind from the tree, the doe scented me and froze. The buck seized the opportunity to catch the doe and trotted in that direction. About halfway to her, he realized something was wrong. Making a half circle, he stopped in a quartering away position, 15 yards from my tree. I had been at full draw because I knew whatever happened was going to happen fast once the doe hit my scent. I was trying to get off a quick shot at the buck when I noticed a small limb that would have deflected my arrow. By squatting as much as possible, I avoided the limb and somehow got my arrow on the way before the buck moved.

The shot looked perfect and the buck ex-

ploded, running hard for the nearby timber. Within seconds, the only reminder of what had just happened was the buck's tracks, a crimson arrow protruding from the snow and my pounding heart. After several reruns in my mind, I climbed down from my stand and admired the coyote for several minutes. Next, I collected my two arrows, taking them to the river to wash and resharpen them before tracking the buck.

The buck's trail was easy to follow and there was no need for more arrows. About 200 yards from my tree, I found my deer, a beautiful whitetail buck that later scored 138 Pope and Young points.

In addition to a little luck, harvesting the coyote required an accurate estimate of the distance and sound shooting ability. A fast-shooting bow helped cover any small error made in estimating the range to the coyote. Because of the close range and size of the buck, it was difficult not to succumb to buck fever. I managed to stay calm, draw at the right time and avoid the small branch that could have caused disaster. Many times, we just think in terms of hitting or missing, but there are always real causes and real cures for our successes and defeats.

HERE IS HOW MOST BOWHUNTERS SHAPE UP:

1. SHOOTING ABILITY—Although not all are successful, most sincere bowhunters make an honest effort to become the best shot possible. Many seem to think their shooting ability alone will get them their game. Being an accurate shot is very helpful in harvesting animals, but it is not the sole consideration.

2. RANGE ESTIMATION—This is an area of weakness for many bowhunters. Stump shooting improves both your ability to judge distance and your shooting ability. I must admit I do

most of my hunting and guiding in the West where shots are more open and consequently longer. Regardless of that fact, range estimation becomes critical after 20 yards. Most bowhunters could improve their overall ability by bringing range estimation into balance with the other aspects of their bowhunting. All it takes is practice.

3. BUCK FEVER—Buck fever is another liability for many bowhunters. It varies so much from individual to individual, however, that it is impossible to make a blanket statement about what approach to use in overcoming the problem. Only you know if you have buck fever and how much it affects your game shooting ability. You must decide what steps you are willing to take to cure the problem. Whatever your choice, remember that buck fever is mental in origin and it can be controlled. For best results, start working on buck fever long before the season opens. This will give you time to build your self-confidence before you encounter that big buck or herd bull.

4. TRAJECTORY—Trajectory, although important, is not affected by your performance at the time of the shot. It is more an aerodynamic function that maximizes your bow and arrow's ability to help you when you make a slight error in range estimation. You make the decision what to do about this situation beforehand. Once this decision is made, it should no longer be an area of concern.

WHY WE MISS

In the final analysis of why shots are missed, shooting ability, trajectory, range estimation and buck fever can all be the cause. At times, it is a combination of these factors. After seeing over 500 arrows released at big game animals, I have drawn the following conclusions.

First, trajectory and range estimation should be combined as a cause because their effects are so closely related. Trajectory and range estimation can be compared to a twin brother and sister. They are similar yet very distinct. If trajectory could be eliminated, accurate range estimation would not be necessary. In other words, you would only need one sight pin for all distances. If the exact yardage was known, trajectory would not be as critical. You would know exactly which sight pin to use for each shot.

Steps that can be taken to improve trajectory and your ability to estimate distances have been discussed and are well worth the effort. My observations indicate that, beyond 25 yards, over 50 percent of missed shots come from this combination of causes.

Without a doubt, the winner in the "causing bowhunters to miss" category is the devil himself, buck fever. When shooting at known distances or at under 25 yards, I would estimate that buck fever is the single most significant cause for missing shots 90 percent of the time. I am surprised by the number of bowhunters who refuse to admit that they have a problem with buck fever. Buck fever is nothing to be ashamed of and appears to be closely tied to the love of hunting. The first step to overcoming buck fever is admitting that it exists.

For some reason, shooting ability catches all the blame for missing when, in reality, it is the only one in the bunch with a white hat. If you can shoot tight groups in the back yard, it has nothing to do with shooting ability when you completely miss a deer at that same distance. If you miss at your maximum effective range or less, shooting ability is not the cause. You don't go out and practice driving just because you ran a red light. Try to prepare as much as possible ahead of time but when you do miss, try your best to identify the cause and then work on that specific aspect of your shooting.

It is this writer's strong belief that the idea of balance should be applied to all aspects of hunting, including those not covered in this book. Some of those areas include the following:

1. Ethics
2. Shot placement
3. Tracking
4. Knowledge of game animals and habitat
5. Scouting
6. Physical conditioning

We all have our strong and weak points as hunters. Some are great stalkers and just seem to have a knack for getting close to animals. Others have unbelievable patience or are accurate game shots. To make the most of your natural abilities, find your strong and weak points from the above and all other aspects of bowhunting. Then put your strong points to work and improve the weak areas. To help illustrate this point, I will use my own case as an example.

My first few seasons of hunting the Colorado mountains taught me many valuable lessons, including this one. Spotting game was not the problem, but what I was seeing was the south end of northbound animals. It didn't take long to figure out that this was not the name of the game for a bowhunter. It was clear that I should slow down and be more careful, but that just didn't seem to work for me.

It soon became apparent that I had to change my methods for getting within bow range of the deer and elk. Then it hit me; I had hunted whitetails from treestands in Pennsylvania. I had also earned my spending money, since age 10, by trapping and was good at reading game sign. My only other strong point was my shooting ability.

Back then, no one I ever heard of had tried to hunt mule deer, much less elk, from treestands. By the same token, there wasn't anyone around to tell me it wouldn't work. At the time, it seemed like the idea to try. After all, I had nothing to lose.

At first the treestands took a great deal of time and effort, but it became evident that, with some refining, the idea would work. After some experimenting with different locations and types of treestands, I found they worked extremely well for both mule deer and elk. In fact, I believe I was one of the first bowhunters in Colorado consistently to harvest elk from treestands. Later, I wrote an article on the subject entitled, "Elk from a Different Angle," *Bowhunter Magazine* (October 1981).

At the same time, I was working to improve my other hunting skills and since that time have taken several deer and elk while stalking and calling. Without even knowing it, I had put my strong points to work, which gave me time to improve on my weak areas. This philosophy of balancing your skills applies to all aspects of bowhunting. By balancing your abilities, you dramatically increase your chances for success.

Spend just a little time around bowhunters and you'll find two points quickly become obvious. Good, close-range shots at big game animals are difficult to come by and each opportunity usually takes a great deal of work, skill and luck to bring about. Second, a high percentage of good shot opportunities are missed each season. If you talk to a bowhunter who has just missed an easy shot, you will be told that, should he have that shot over, he would not miss again. Many times, that is probably a true statement. The point, however, is that we don't often get that second chance. The only answer is to be prepared before your shooting opportunities arrive. Be a balanced bowhunter.

This bull and his cows were located while glassing a ridge. While the bull worked over a small tree, I stalked within range.

My second deer taken with the bow. As I grow older, pictures mean more than ever; they help me relive some wonderful hunts.

A whitetail buck and a coyote. What a morning!

The most popular way to take antelope is from blinds near water holes.

In my opinion, old mule deer bucks are one of the most difficult animals to bowhunt.

Mountain goats inhabit extremely rugged terrain but they are not as wary as some other species.

A spike bull shot from a treestand. Treestands can be effective but you need to know the elk's habits and the terrain very well.

Most whitetails are taken from treestands. I almost froze to death waiting for this old boy to move within bow range.

Antelope can also be taken by spotting and stalking. This method works best in rugged terrain.

My largest whitetail taken from the ground. I was just plain lucky on this one.

Small game hunting is a great way to improve hunting skills and have fun at the same time.

A nice bull that came in silently to investigate my bugling.

When dogs are used to hunt mountain lions, the chase is often physically demanding and exciting.

A friend called this bull in for me during an evening hunt. Teaming up to hunt elk can be effective.

This bird was shot in the fall but the most popular time to hunt turkeys is in the spring.

The dog was upset because he didn't get to go along on this hunt.

A large-bodied bull taken from a treestand with a 25-yard shot.

Colorado and a few other Western states open the archery season while the deer are still in velvet.

THE COMPOUND BOW AT WORK 6

Choosing new equipment can be very confusing and frustrating. Without looking far, you can find a convincing advocate for every brand name of bow made. No wonder it's difficult. The truth is most bows will get the job done, but they are not all created equal. The purpose of this chapter is to expand your knowledge of a "bow at work" and give you valuable insight into what factors affect arrow speed and bow performance. This knowledge will help you get the most from your present bow or help you select new equipment that is right for you.

Human nature is such that most of us will enjoy any bow we shoot. After a period of time, it is easy to believe we made the best possible choice. I made this error a few years after compounds arrived on the market. By choosing a top brand name and the most expensive model, I was convinced my bow was the best made. I enjoyed hunting with the bow and was successful; however, it took me two years to realize my mistake. My bow was not inadequate or terrible, but I could have chosen

a much better performing bow and, in this case, saved money at the same time. Elements hidden within a bow's design can and do affect its overall performance. Some are not detectable even to the most experienced bowhunter without proper investigation.

To provide a standard for testing and comparing bows, the Archery Manufacturers Organization (AMO) has set the following specifications:

- 60-pound draw weight
- 30-inch draw length
- 540-grain arrow

A bow meeting these exact specifications will be referred to in this text as the AMO standard or an AMO bow and the 540-grain arrow may at times be called an AMO arrow. The speed at which an AMO bow shoots a 540-grain arrow is known as the rating velocity. The rating velocity is given in feet per second (FPS), (i.e., the rating velocity of this bow is 216 FPS).

When administered correctly, this is a fair test by which to compare one bow to another in regard to arrow speed. You could say that the AMO standard helps the consumer compare apples with apples. But alone, even the AMO standard doesn't tell the whole story.

Two major elements affect arrow speed: (1) the amount of energy a bow stores in its limbs as the string is being pulled to full draw, and (2) how efficiently a bow delivers that stored energy to the arrow when the string is released.

Regardless of a bow's design, energy is stored in the limbs as you draw the bow. When the string is released, most of that stored energy is transferred to the arrow as it is propelled forward. Of the energy not absorbed by the arrow, the majority goes to move the mass weight of the limbs, cams, cables, string, etc. The remainder goes to friction, noise and vibration.

Where does the energy that a bow stores come from? The stored energy comes from your body as you draw the bow. Most of the effort you exert while pulling the string is stored in the limbs of the bow. As just mentioned, when the string is released the majority of that stored energy is transferred to the arrow. Absorbing this energy causes the arrow to be propelled through the air. The arrow delivers to the target much of the energy you originally exerted when drawing the bow. At the point the arrow left the bow, the stored energy was converted to kinetic energy (energy of motion). The more kinetic energy an arrow possesses, the harder it will hit (penetrate).

The amount of energy stored by a bow is largely determined by the number of pounds you pull (draw weight), the distance you pull those pounds (draw length) and the design (shape) of the cam. To qualify the term "cam," you need to understand that a round wheel is also a cam. Round wheel is only one name used to describe a certain cam design. "Cam"

will be used in this text as a general term when discussing all types of wheels and cams. Three names will be used when referring to a "specific cam design": the *high-energy cam,* the *modified cam* and the *round wheel.*

Cams do not themselves store energy, but their design has a large influence on the amount of energy a bow stores in its limbs. A bow equipped with high-energy cams, for example, will shoot an arrow faster than a round wheel bow only because it has stored additional energy (your extra effort) in the limbs. There is no magic; the energy that a bow transfers to the arrow upon release was put there by the person who drew the bow. When one bow shoots an arrow faster than another, there is a concrete reason for the additional speed. In other words, "You don't get what you don't pay for."

When choosing a compound bow, you must choose a draw weight and draw length that are right for you. Most of today's bows have adjustable draw weights and draw lengths. The cam design of most bows is not adjustable and consequently should be evaluated carefully before purchasing. Compound bow manufacturers use a multitude of names for these "cams," such as round wheels, energy wheels, programmed cams, high-energy cams and many more. Each manufacturer chooses a name for his particular cam design, but unfortunately, the name doesn't always accurately represent that design.

To illustrate how cam design affects a bow's ability to store energy, I have listed, in foot pounds, the amount of energy the three types of cams mentioned earlier would cause a bow to store (figure 17). To compare these differences, we will assume all bows are set to AMO standards (i.e., a 30-inch draw length, 60-pound bow).

1. The round wheel would cause about 60

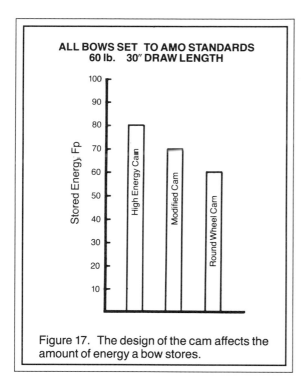

ALL BOWS SET TO AMO STANDARDS
60 lb. 30″ DRAW LENGTH

Figure 17. The design of the cam affects the amount of energy a bow stores.

energy, the high-energy cam bow could require a stiffer spined arrow if both bows were set at the same draw weight. This is a point to keep in mind when you choose your arrows, particularly if you shoot a modified or high-energy cam bow.

A graph of a force-draw curve is a picture of a bow storing the energy we have been discussing in its limbs as the string is being drawn. The force-draw curve of a round wheel starts upward at a sharp angle, reaching a peak (its draw weight) just beyond the midway point of the draw (figure 18). It stays at peak weight for approximately one inch then drops off evenly to the valley (its holding weight). The valley is approximately one inch in width. If you draw a compound bow beyond the valley (its set draw length), the draw weight rises rapidly because you are pulling against what is referred to as "the wall." This could damage your bow and is a good reason for not allowing

foot pounds of energy to be stored in the limbs of the bow.

2. An average modified cam would cause 70 foot pounds of energy to be stored.
3. A high-energy cam would cause approximately 80 foot pounds of energy to be stored.

The reason 70 foot pounds of stored energy was used to represent the modified cam is that it is the middle ground between the round wheel and the high-energy cam. In reality the amount of energy a "modified cam" causes to be stored could be anywhere between a round wheel and a high-energy cam.

As you can see from these examples, a 60-pound high-energy cam bow could store as much energy as an 80-pound round wheel bow. In real terms, this means the 60-pound bow could shoot an arrow just as fast as the 80 pounder. Because of the difference in stored

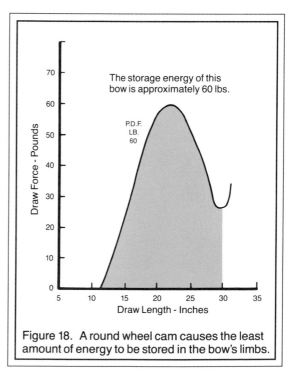

The storage energy of this bow is approximately 60 lbs.

P.D.F.
LB.
60

Figure 18. A round wheel cam causes the least amount of energy to be stored in the bow's limbs.

a stranger to draw your bow unless his draw length is the same or less than your own.

The force-draw curve of a high-energy cam starts up more sharply than does the round wheel (figure 19). It will remain at the peak draw weight for several inches, then drop off rapidly to the valley (its holding weight). Because of the sharper drop off, the cam bow has a narrower valley, making it more sensitive to an exact draw length. The cam bow delivers a more rapid rise and fall of stored energy to the arrow when the string is released. This can cause vibrations in the system. These two points make a cam bow a little more difficult to shoot accurately.

Before you decide that you want a cam bow that stores the maximum amount of energy (a high-energy cam bow), you should be aware of the possible disadvantages. As a general rule, bows with high-energy cams are more difficult to draw, noisier and have a rougher "in the

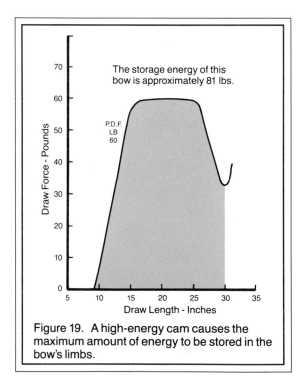

Figure 19. A high-energy cam causes the maximum amount of energy to be stored in the bow's limbs.

hand" feel after the shot. They are often more critical to shoot, less efficient and more stressful to the other bow parts, such as limbs, cables, strings, etc. The advantage of high-energy cam bows is that they store more energy and consequently shoot a faster arrow. As a general rule, an AMO high-energy cam bow will shoot an arrow approximately 18 FPS faster than an AMO round wheel bow when the arrow weight is the same.

The round wheel bow takes less effort to draw and shoot. It is also more forgiving and it is less stressful to the limbs, string, cables and riser. On the negative side, the round wheel does not cause as much energy to be stored in the limbs. This difference in stored energy ensures that a round wheel bow will not shoot an arrow as fast as a high-energy cam bow when both meet AMO standards.

When considering only arrow speed, it is unfair to compare a round wheel bow with a high-energy cam bow. The opposite is true when you are considering shooting pleasure, stability, accuracy and noise. Something akin to shooting magnum rifles, pistols and shotguns, there are advantages and disadvantages to shooting a high-energy cam bow. You must choose what is most important to you.

The modified cam that stored 70 foot pounds of energy in the earlier example would be a compromise between a high-energy cam and a round wheel bow (figure 20). It has been my experience that modified cam bows maintain many of the smooth shooting qualities of round wheel bows, while adding extra stored energy. I find an AMO bow (60 pounds, 30-inch draw) that stores between 68 and 74 foot pounds of energy to be an excellent compromise for hunting bows.

Once again, when considering a new bow, don't be fooled by the name of the cam. Ask how much energy the model bow you are considering will store when set to AMO stan-

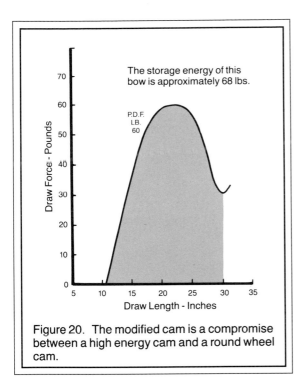

Figure 20. The modified cam is a compromise between a high energy cam and a round wheel cam.

this important information.

Archery World Magazine offers a comprehensive "Bow Report" in each issue. The bow reports are compiled by Norb Mullaney, a highly respected engineer from Milwaukee, Wisconsin. The information in these reports is the most comprehensive available today and is extremely informative. The reports can be helpful when choosing a new bow or increasing your general knowledge about bow performance. Some important points to consider in the bow reports are: the force-draw curve, bow efficiency, the amount of stored energy, the rating velocity and Mr. Mullaney's commentary. Bow reports on previously tested models are available from *Archery World Magazine* while the supply lasts. There is a charge for each report. Contact *Archery World* for the particulars.

DRAW WEIGHT REDUCTION

The cam design and the amount of draw weight reduction are both predetermined by the manufacturer. The draw weight reduction or let-off, in simplified terms, is controlled by how near the edge of the cam the axle hole is placed. When the bow is assembled, the let-off is also affected by the rigging or set-up. The reduction in holding weight of today's compound bows varies between 35 and 75 percent. An average reduction would be approximately 50 percent. This figure does vary, so be sure to check the manufacturer's specifications. A shooter using a 60-pound peak weight bow with a 50-percent let-off would be holding 30 pounds in the valley (at full draw).

As a general rule, when comparing bows of equal design a higher let-off bow will store less energy. In addition, my experience has shown that most shooters can comfortably hold approximately 50 percent of any peak weight they can draw. At the risk of stepping on a few toes,

dards. Unfortunately, you will find this information difficult to obtain. Most sales personnel and many manufacturers are unable (or unwilling) to answer the stored energy question. The best place to locate this and other helpful information will be given shortly. Although important, the energy storing ability of a bow is just one point to consider when making that final choice.

Another point to consider is that different bows store energy at different times during the draw. Bows can have different appearing force-draw curves even when they ultimately store about the same amount of energy. A bow that has a smooth rounded force-draw curve (figure 20 above) should likewise have a smooth feel as you pull the string to full draw. Before choosing a bow, it is important that you see its force-draw curve and know its energy storage ability. You should also shoot the bow before making a final decision. Now, where to find

I would say that draw weight reduction in excess of 60 percent is not necessary. In addition, if you reduce the holding weight too much, you may have a difficult time achieving a clean, crisp release, especially with fingers. On the other hand, a possible advantage to high let-off bows is that the lower holding weight may help some shooters control target panic and buck fever.

Here is one side note in this regard: high let-off bows are not any easier to pull to the peak weight as one manufacturer implies. *Seventy-five pounds is still 75 pounds.* They only become easier to pull once you have drawn beyond the peak weight of the bow.

ARROW SPEED

You often hear a bowhunter or salesman quote a superfast arrow speed for a certain bow. It is very important to understand that this information alone can be misleading. Several elements affect arrow speed, regardless of the quality of the individual bow. In other words, anyone can make you think a certain bow is fast by not giving you all the necessary information. If a person quotes you the arrow speed of a bow without including the draw weight, draw length and arrow weight, ask for this additional information. If that individual does not know the answers to these important questions, he is not knowledgeable about the elements that affect arrow speed or is intentionally trying to mislead you.

The speed at which a bow shoots an arrow is affected by: (1) the draw weight, (2) the power stroke, (3) the arrow weight and (4) the bow's efficiency. These elements and their effect on arrow speed are discussed below. The data presented are averages for normal weight hunting arrows and are intended to give you a general idea of how each element affects arrow speed. These figures will vary slightly from bow to bow.

DRAW WEIGHT

Draw weight affects arrow speed approximately 1¾ FPS (for mid-range arrow weights) per pound of draw weight added or subtracted. A bow shoots an arrow faster when the draw weight is increased because it causes the bow to store more energy. For example, if you add 5 pounds to the draw weight of your bow, it will increase the arrow speed by approximately 9 FPS. The opposite occurs when the draw weight is reduced. Within reason, the starting point is irrelevant.

THE POWER STROKE

The power stroke is the distance the bow is delivering force or power to the arrow upon release of the string. Two elements affect the power stroke of a bow: the shooter's draw length and the brace height. The brace height is set to a large degree by a bow's design, but it is also affected by changes in string length. Using a longer string lowers the brace height. A shorter string has the opposite effect. Regardless of these factors, the shooter's draw length is by far the dominant element in determining the power stroke of a bow.

The draw length of a bow is determined by bow design, the rigging, the string length, cam diameter and design. Your draw length is determined by your physical size, shooting style and anchor point. It is very important to match a bow's draw length to your specific draw length. There are two standards for measuring draw length: the true draw method and the AMO standard. Please refer to the chapter on "Bows and Strings" for a full explanation of draw length.

The arrow speed will change approximately 5 FPS for each inch the draw length is increased or decreased from the AMO standard of 30 inches. To help understand why, let us compare two compound bows exactly alike with a 10-inch brace height (figure 21). One bow is set for a 28-inch draw length and the other is set for a 32-inch draw length. Assuming we have the correct size shooter for each bow, the 28-inch draw length bow has an 18-inch power stroke (28 inches less the 10-inch brace height). The 32-inch bow has 4 additional inches to store energy as the bow is being drawn. This gives the 32-inch draw length bow a 22-inch power stroke. The arrow from the 32-inch draw length bow will be moving approximately 20 FPS faster than the arrow from the 28-inch draw length bow if all other factors remain equal. But the 32-inch draw length bow would require a longer and higher spined arrow shaft. These two considerations would increase the total arrow weight and reduce the gain in arrow speed.

The change for a recurve bow would be approximately the same if the draw weight for both bows was the same at the respective draw lengths. An example would be: one bow 60 pounds at a 28-inch draw length, the second bow 60 pounds at a 32-inch draw length. Again, the person shooting the 60-pound recurve at 32 inches would be shooting a faster arrow.

This doesn't seem fair to those of us with short draw lengths. This is particularly true for women who usually have shorter draw lengths than men. One solution is to add draw weight. Here again, more women than men are at a disadvantage because of strength limitations. These realities seem unfair to female bowhunters and can make it more difficult for them to shoot arrows with substantial kinetic energy to harvest large animals such as elk and moose. If you are a female bowhunter, don't allow this information to discourage you. Shari Fraker is a petite, well-known, Colorado bow-

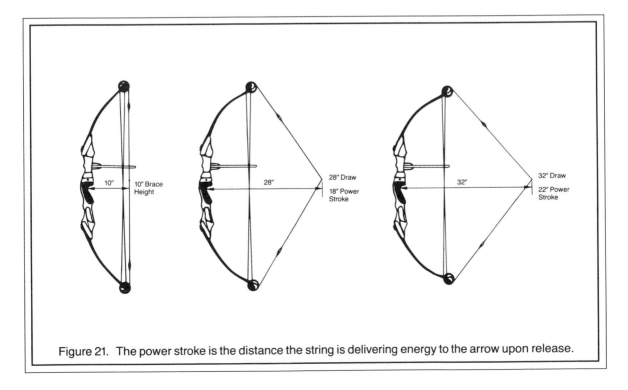

Figure 21. The power stroke is the distance the string is delivering energy to the arrow upon release.

hunter who has harvested many elk with what could be considered lightweight bowhunting equipment. If you are forced to use lightweight equipment, you should be especially cautious about shot angles. Mrs. Fraker is a shot placement instructor and is much in favor of the broadside shot on large animals.

Here are a few suggestions for those who may be small in stature or have strength limitations. First, it is important to everyone, but even more important for a person with these limitations, to choose an efficient model bow. Second, for hunters who use under a 55-pound bow on large animals, I would recommend trying a modified or high-energy cam bow. This would add kinetic energy (penetrating potential) to your arrow at a time when it is approaching the critical level for the larger animals. As a side benefit, it would also reduce trajectory. In all cases, do so only if you find a bow you can shoot accurately. Finally, if you have a short draw length, do not try to increase it by overdrawing your bow. We all have a natural draw length, and chances are it should not be changed. If you overdraw your bow, it could have serious effects on your shooting accuracy.

ARROW WEIGHT

A 25-grain change in arrow weight will change the arrow velocity approximately 4 FPS. A 100-grain change in arrow weight effects a 16 FPS change in arrow speed. This same 100-grain change in arrow weight also effects a 2½-percent change in the bow's efficiency. This will be covered in greater detail below. See the chapter on "The Arrow" for ideas on how to reduce arrow weight.

BOW EFFICIENCY

Bow efficiency is a hidden element in arrow speed and one often overlooked by the bowhunter. The percentage of a bow's stored energy delivered to the arrow is what determines its efficiency. When two bows are equal in stored energy and draw length, the more efficient bow will shoot the faster arrow. The amount of stored energy delivered to the arrow by compound bows varies between 60 and 85 percent. That is a 25-percent difference. Even top of the line brand name bows can vary up to 10 percent in efficiency and that can amount to 15 FPS in arrow speed.

This brings up a good argument for choosing an efficient bow (figure 22). For example, we have two 60-pound high-energy cam bows that both store 77 foot pounds of energy in their limbs. Bow Number One has an efficiency rating of 68 percent and will shoot its 540-grain arrow at 210 FPS. It will also have the 24½ foot pounds of energy not absorbed by the arrow, going back into the bow. This energy will be dispersed in the form of noise, vibration, friction, etc. Bow Number Two has an efficiency rating of 78 percent and will shoot its 540-grain arrow at 225 FPS. It will have only 17 foot pounds of unused energy going back into the bow. Bow Number Two shoots a faster arrow and there is less wasted energy. Chances are Bow Number Two will also be more pleasant to shoot.

Your effort is what puts the stored energy we have been discussing into the bow. An efficient bow will return you more of that energy in the form of arrow speed. In regard to a bow storing energy, the point was made earlier that "you don't get what you don't pay for." When it comes to delivering that stored energy to the arrow, you may not get "what you did pay for." For this reason, bow efficiency is a very important consideration when choosing a new bow. Unfortunately, it is difficult for the average consumer to determine the amount of energy a bow stores in its limbs and then find what

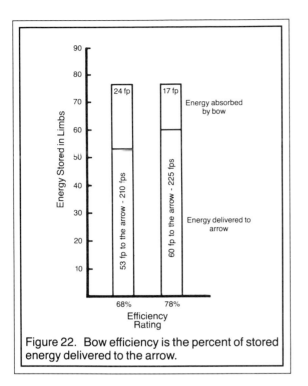

Figure 22. Bow efficiency is the percent of stored energy delivered to the arrow.

percent of that energy is delivered to the arrow (bow efficiency). Again, the best place the consumer can get an assessment of a bow's efficiency is in *Archery World*'s "Bow Report."

A bow's efficiency is affected by the combined weight of the limbs, wheels, cables, bow string, friction and bow design. Bow efficiency is also affected by a change in the arrow's weight. When you reduce arrow weight 100 grains, the efficiency of the bow is reduced by approximately 2½ percent. Regardless of this fact, arrow speed is still increased by 16 FPS. That increase would flatten trajectory approximately 15 percent when starting with an arrow speed of 200 FPS.

One negative effect of reducing arrow weight is that this additional unused energy causes a little more noise and vibration in the bow. An extreme example of this would be shooting zero arrow weight which would equal a dry fire (releasing the bow from full draw without an arrow on the string). In a complete dry fire, all the stored energy is transferred back into the bow violently and could cause serious damage including breaking the limbs. Reducing the arrow's weight too much is like causing a partial dry fire for each shot.

When starting in the normal arrow weight range, 2½ percent more energy going back into the bow should not cause a problem. To help prevent damage to the bow, however, there should be a limit. Most experts recommend arrow weight based on draw weight, but, as pointed out in this chapter, bows of the same draw weight can vary widely in the amount of energy they store. For this reason, the amount of energy a bow stores should be a consideration when choosing arrow weight.

My choice is a compromise between heavy and extremely lightweight arrows. I would, however, suggest never going below 7 grains of arrow weight per pound of draw weight regardless of cam design. Due to spine requirements, you may not have total control over your arrow weight unless you shoot an overdraw.

BOW PERFORMANCE

Bow performance should not be confused with bow efficiency. Bow performance includes all aspects of how a bow performs. These include bow efficiency, arrow speed, accuracy, durability, noise level, the shooter's comfort, etc. Even price can be included in this list because we each have a limit to what we feel performance is worth. When choosing from this list, you will be forced to make compromises.

Overall performance can be somewhat subjective because we don't all place the same importance on each individual area. That is one reason there are so many makes and models of bows on the market.

ARROW SPEED DETERMINATION

There is a way to determine your approximate arrow speed without the use of a chronograph. The information in this section will also show you the results when there is a change in draw weight, arrow weight and type of bow—changes many bowhunters consider making from time to time. Now you can see these effects on arrow speed without actually making the change.

First, we need a standard from which to make the adjustments. The AMO example bow will serve that purpose. The bow we are using for our standard is a top of the line, *30*-inch draw, *60*-pound, *high-energy cam* bow, with *average efficiency,* shooting a *540*-grain arrow. The rating velocity of this AMO bow is **216** FPS. This is the number from which we will be making our adjustments.

Each time your equipment doesn't match an italicized item of the example bow exactly, refer to factors 1 through 6. Then add or subtract the suggested amount from the 216 FPS. This will give you the approximate arrow speed of your bow as it is set up for you. An example will be given.

ADJUSTMENT FACTORS

1. Draw weight: Arrow speed will increase or decrease approximately 1¾ FPS for each 1-pound change in draw weight over or under 60 pounds, respectively.
2. Draw length: Arrow speed will change 5 FPS for each inch of draw length change (add for over 30-inch draw and subtract for under 30-inch draw).
3. Arrow weight: Arrow speed will decrease or increase approximately 4 FPS for each 25-grain change in arrow weight over or under 540 grains, respectively.

4. Modified cam: Reduce arrow speed 9 FPS. In reality, modified cams vary considerably. The amount of energy they cause a bow to store may be anywhere between that of a round wheel and a high-energy cam. Unless you have additional information to make a more accurate estimation, subtract the suggested 9 FPS.
5. Round wheel: Reduce arrow speed 18 FPS for a round wheel bow.
6. Bow efficiency: Has been adjusted to an average level through AMO example bow's arrow speed. If you are sure you have a very efficient bow, add *up to 8 FPS,* or subtract *up to 8 FPS* for an extremely inefficient bow.

To calculate your bow's approximate arrow speed, compare it to the example bow. Then make the necessary changes from the above list of adjustment factors. Below is an example that runs through the procedure.

Problem: You want to find the approximate arrow speed of your top of the line, round wheel bow set at 65 pounds. Your draw length is 31 inches and your arrow weight is 565 grains.

This method of finding the arrow speed of a given bow is usually accurate within plus or minus 10 FPS. Arrow speed will also fluctuate depending on the use of fingers or a release and how much your draw length changes from shot to shot.

The process for determining a bow's arrow speed is shorter and more exact when you know rating velocity for the model bow in question. This information eliminates the need to estimate the amount of energy a bow stores (round wheel modified cam or high-energy cam). It also eliminates the need to estimate the bow's efficiency. When you know the rating velocity, the process described for determining arrow speed is usually accurate within 5 FPS.

ADJUSTMENT EXAMPLE

Adjustment factors	Adjustment needed
1. Draw weight:	Add 9 FPS.
2. Draw length:	Add 5 FPS.
3. Arrow weight:	Subtract 4 FPS.
4. Modified cam:	Not applicable with this bow.
5. Round wheel:	Subtract 18 FPS.
6. Bow efficiency:	No change with this bow.

The example AMO bow started with .... 216 FPS.

Round wheel and arrow weight factors .... -22 FPS.

Draw weight and draw length factors .... + 14 FPS.

Your 65# bow shoots the 565-gr. arrow at .... 208 FPS.

Unfortunately, most manufacturers do not give the rating velocity of their bows. Your best bet is the "Bow Report," but these reports are not available on all makes and models. **When you do know the rating velocity, proceed as in the example problem but use only adjustment factors 1 through 3**.

After arriving at your approximate arrow speed, refer to the trajectory chart in the chapter on "Trajectory" to see the number of inches you would shoot low if you made a 5-yard error in range estimation. As you can see by the above example, a bow that shoots a 540-grain arrow at 240 FPS is rare, regardless of what you might be told. This is especially true of round wheel bows. A few bowhunters do shoot their arrows over 250 FPS but this much arrow speed often requires a heavyweight, high-energy cam bow with an overdraw system and light arrows. These set-ups are often very stressful to the bow and critical to shoot.

My observations and work with the chronograph show the average bowhunter's arrow speed to be in the 190 FPS range. When starting with this figure, arrow speed can be improved rather dramatically. Do not think you must reach a certain number. *Any* increase in arrow speed will help flatten the trajectory path of your arrow.

Arrow speed and bow efficiency are certainly not the only considerations when purchasing a new bow, but they should be given due consideration. Not all bows are created equal.

Here are a few more general guidelines to help you choose a bow. If you are concerned with bow efficiency and performance, choose from top of the line model bows. This fact alone does not guarantee anything, but it does improve your chances of getting a more efficient, better performing bow. If the local archery shop has a chronograph, test your old bow against the new bow you are considering. Check each bow's draw weight and make the necessary adjustments before the test. Make sure you use the same arrows in both bows. If you use more than one arrow, they must be the same weight and length.

A mistake many bowhunters make when shooting through a chronograph is to "overdraw" the bow (pull against the wall on a compound bow). If you have occasion to shoot your bow through a chronograph, do not overdraw. Shoot the bow like you normally would. You are after the truth, not an inflated number that means nothing.

There are many important elements to consider when purchasing a new bow. Bows are expensive and you don't want to make a mistake. Spend time shooting any bow you intend to purchase. The information in this and the following chapter, "The Bow and String," will help you choose a bow that better fits your individual needs as a bowhunter.

THE BOW AND STRING 7

The bow was developed as a prehistoric tool around 30,000 B.C. It revolutionized hunting methods by allowing prehistoric man to harvest game at greater distances than previously possible with the spear.

Beginning about 5,000 B.C., the Egyptians were the first organized society to use the bow. They utilized the bow and arrow for both hunting and war. Approximately A.D. 900 the Turks developed recurve and laminated limb bows. Their laminated limbs were made from wood, horn and tendon.

The bow was the chief weapon during the One Hundred Years' war which began in A.D. 1337. At the battle of Agincourt in 1415, 13,000 English soldiers armed with long bows defeated 50,000 French troops.

The first archery instructional book was published during the 1540s. Oddly enough, about this same time the gun was rapidly replacing the bow as the weapon of choice in Europe. The invention of gunpowder greatly reduced the use and further development of the bow

by advanced societies until the 20th century.

Slowly, a renewed interest began in America during the late 1800s with men like Maurice and Will Thompson. The interest continued into this century with men like Saxton Pope, Art Young, Fred Bear, Howard Hill and many others. By the 1930s, there was enough interest from the general public to support small archery companies. With these companies, led by Bear Archery, came new developments, such as solid fiberglass bows, new glues, wood and fiberglass laminated limbs, etc. The sport grew slowly but steadily into the 1960s.

In the way of technology, the next major development was the invention of the compound bow by H. W. Allen in 1966. The compound bow created great interest and controversy. Despite considerable protest, compound bows were legalized for hunting in most states by the mid-1970s.

Archery was adopted as an Olympic medal sport beginning with the 1972 summer games. The combination of archery becoming an official Olympic sport and the development of the compound bow spurred tremendous growth in competitive archery and bowhunting from the mid-'70s through the early '80s. At this time, the growth has stabilized in most areas. Even though the compound bow has been around for two decades, its pros and cons are still hotly debated in some circles.

It is beyond the scope of this book to address the equipment controversy. The issues concerning equipment choices were well addressed by Dwight Schuh in his article entitled "The Great Bow Debate" (*Bowhunter Magazine,* February/March 1988).

This chapter will deal primarily with compound bows because they offer such a wide variety of choices and are the least understood. Each bow part will be discussed with special emphasis placed upon the positive and negative effects of material and design changes. When choosing a bow, you may be forced to make compromises between cost, performance, accuracy, speed, noise, dependability, etc. Seldom are the issues black and white. The purpose of the first part of this chapter is to help equip you with basic knowledge of bow construction so you can make an informed bow choice.

DRAW LENGTH

If you were to take several different compound bows marked for 30-inch draw lengths by their manufacturers, you would find they may vary in draw length up to one inch or more. This fact alone does not cause a problem because, like bows, bowhunters do not come in even one-inch draw lengths. It is, however, very important to match the bow's draw length to the draw length of the shooter.

Two terms are used when discussing draw length, and it is helpful to understand both. The first is referred to as the "true draw method."

The second is the standard set by the Archery Manufacturers Organization (AMO). The AMO method simply adds 1¾ inches to the true draw number (figure 23). These two measurements are used for different purposes as will be explained.

Draw length is the distance from the nocking point to the cushion plunger hole in the riser when the shooter is at full draw. More specifically, this measurement is from the nocking point to the low or contact point of the grip. To accomplish the actual measuring, take an old arrow and have a friend mark it exactly at the cushion plunger with a magic marker when you are at full draw. Repeat the process several times and take an average if your draw length is not consistent. If your bow does not have a cushion plunger hole, mark the arrow directly above the place where your hand contacts the grip (the low point). If the cushion plunger hole is not directly above the low point of the

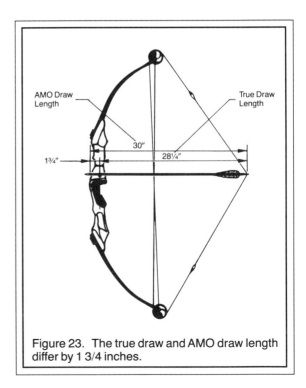

Figure 23. The true draw and AMO draw length differ by 1 3/4 inches.

grip, make the proper adjustment when marking the arrow.

To find your correct draw length, you need to assume the correct shooting stance and have a solid anchor point. A factor to be aware of when checking your draw length on a compound bow is that most shooters will unknowingly make small adjustments in their draw length to find the valley. This is natural because the draw weight is at its lowest point in the valley and your body will automatically make minor adjustments to find the point of least resistance. To ensure that you find your correct draw length, measure it on several different bows. For example, if you believe your draw length is about 30 inches, try a 29-, 30- and 31-inch bow. Also try a very light draw weight recurve bow if available. The idea is to find your exact draw length. If you are new to archery, take into account that your draw length may increase slightly as you become more familiar with shooting. Your draw length may also change slightly (usually shorter) if you change to a release.

After you find your true draw length, record the number and save the marked arrow. Use this arrow to check or adjust the draw length of all future bows. The true draw measurement, or better yet, your marked arrow, should be used to make sure a bow is set to your correct draw length. As mentioned, some new bows will not be the exact draw length they are marked. Your marked arrow should also be used when making small adjustments to a bow's draw length.

As mentioned above, to determine your AMO draw length, add 1¾ inches to your true draw length measurement (as above). Bows come from the factory set according to the AMO draw length standard. It is important to remember that you will be using the AMO draw length when ordering or purchasing a bow and determining your arrow length.

But to ensure that all future bows are set to your exact draw length, use the true draw measurement. Again make sure you keep an arrow marked with your draw length and write this measurement down. When using the above method for setting a bow's draw length, you dictate your draw length to the bow, not vice versa, and your draw length will remain the same from bow to bow. The reason for such fine detail is that draw length variations can affect your shooting accuracy.

In recent years, many compound bows have been equipped with "tri-draw round wheels" allowing for three 1-inch changes in draw length. Many modified and high-energy cams have interchangeable draw length modules for 1-inch changes in draw length. Some also offer the tri-draw configuration. These types of adjustments should get you within one-half inch or less of the correct draw length, assuming you started with the proper sized cam. From this point, the bow can be fine tuned as to draw length by changing string length. A ½-inch change in string length will change the draw length approximately ¾ inch. This figure is only an average and it will vary from bow to bow. Another point to be aware of is that shortening the draw length will usually reduce the draw weight slightly. Increasing the draw length has the opposite effect.

The first step in adjusting a new bow to your draw length is to make any adjustments provided for in the cams until the new bow is as close as possible to the correct draw length. Some bows also provide for minor adjustments by including different length slots in the grommet located in the cable yoke system. This grommet is sometimes called a cable yoke adjuster. If you are lucky, the bow's combined adjustments will suffice and your bow will not need any further draw length modification. If this is the case, make sure you record the string length and purchase two extra strings. "Shoot in" the new strings to make sure they stretch to the correct length.

If you are not so lucky, or your cams do not provide for adjustments, the best way to fine tune the draw length is with small changes in the string length. To accomplish this, you will more than likely need an odd-length string, such as 40¼ inches. This will necessitate purchasing custom-made strings (see the section on custom-made strings in this chapter). This may be the only way to maintain a consistent draw length when changing bows. Most bows should not have their draw length adjusted more than 1 inch by changing the string length. If more draw length adjustment is needed, a change in wheel or cam size would be in order.

CHOOSING A CAM

When purchasing a new bow, the type of cam you choose should be given careful consideration because the amount of energy cams cause the bow to store varies so greatly. The advantages and disadvantages of round wheels and of modified and high-energy cams were covered in the chapter on "The Compound Bow at Work."

The cams themselves are made from either high-impact, molded substances (such as nylon and plastic) or lightweight, alloy metals. The alloy metal wheels and cams are generally lighter and consequently accepted as the present state of the art. Most manufacturers equip their top of the line bows with alloy metal cams. But a few bows with molded cams are very impressive with regard to overall performance, especially if you factor in the reduced cost.

When considering a new bow, you should always check for cam lean (figure 24). The best way to check for cam lean is with the bow at full draw. Simply look up at the top cam and see if it appears to be straight up and down. Severe cam lean will also cause the cable to turn and possibly to leave its groove. To check the bottom cam, turn the bow over, draw it upside down and follow the same procedure.

Although manufacturers, engineers and archers will argue about the amount of negative effect cam lean will have on the bow, most will agree that it is not a benefit. Some manufacturers use cable yoke systems to help prevent cam lean.

To me, cam lean is a sign of system torque and/or poor bearing fit, etc. Whatever the cause, it serves no beneficial purpose. How much negative effect it has, I honestly don't know, but again, it may be something you want to check before spending your hard-earned money on a new bow. At any rate, always try a new bow before buying it, especially if you are changing from a round wheel bow to a modified or high-energy cam bow.

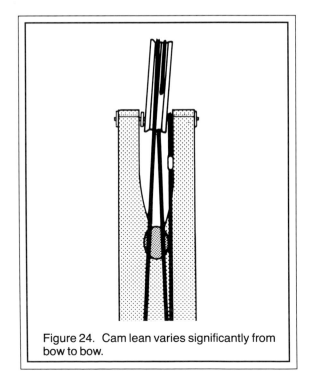

Figure 24. Cam lean varies significantly from bow to bow.

THE LIMBS

The bow limbs, referred to as fiberglass by most bowhunters, are actually filament reinforced plastic, or more simply FRP. Filament reinforced plastic limbs can withstand more stress than wood laminated limbs and, as a result, they will generally last longer under the same conditions. They are also less expensive to produce. These two facts allow manufacturers to produce a less expensive bow, both from the initial cost aspect and future warranty liability.

One negative aspect of FRP limbs is their physical weight. They are normally double the weight of an equal sized wood laminated limb. Because of this weight factor, more of the bow's energy goes toward starting the heavier limb into motion. Depending on bow design, you often get a rougher "in the hand" feel after the shot as the heavier limbs come to a stop.

Wood laminated limbs are generally more efficient than FRP limbs. Consequently, they are likely to shoot a faster arrow when bow design is the same. A bow with laminated limbs will usually not feel as rough in your hand after the shot. On the negative side, they will raise the cost of the bow and may have a shorter life.

Some manufacturers will go to a great deal of effort to convince you that their FRP limbs are just as fast as wood laminated limbs. Unless the FRP limb is stressed more through a slight design change in the bow, that statement is suspect. After testing many bows, I have found that the wood laminated limb bows do usually shoot faster and have a smoother feel than FRP limb bows. This is an equipment choice you must make and another of the many important reasons to shoot and compare bows before buying one.

The above does not mean that bows equipped with FRP limbs should be ignored. They do have their strong points as mentioned—strength and cost. Bow design has a large influence on the amount of stress placed on the limbs. Because FRP limbs can withstand more stress, they are the obvious choice for certain designs, such as short-limb, high-energy cam bows. Manufacturers have continually improved FRP limbs and, in the future, they may surpass the wood laminated limbs in all respects.

RISERS (HANDLES)

At first glance, you might wonder what can be different about risers. When choosing a new bow, most bowhunters' primary concerns about the riser are:

1. The grip—comfort and fit
2. The sight window—size
3. Overall aesthetics—looks

These points are certainly important considerations in choosing the type of bow riser that suits your needs. But there are additional elements about risers that you may want to consider the next time you purchase a bow.

RISER DESIGN

A deflexed design riser is generally known for adding stability to a bow's design. The reflex riser design usually improves the bow's ability to store energy by lowering its brace height thus increasing the power stroke. Here's how to tell the differences in design of a riser.

Use a long straight object; an arrow will work. Hold the arrow parallel against the riser so that the nock end of the arrow touches the riser at the exact point where the upper limb leaves the riser. The point end of the arrow should then touch the riser at the exact point the bottom limb leaves the riser. Lay the bow on the floor with the sight window side up and the arrow touching both points mentioned (figure 25). If the contact point of the grip (approximately the cushion plunger hole on most bows) is in front of the shaft, you have a deflexed riser. If the contact point of the grip is on the string side of the shaft, you have a reflex riser. As a general rule, a bow with a deflexed riser design will have a higher brace height.

My personal preference is a slightly deflexed riser. As long as you do not go to an extreme in either direction, this factor alone will not have a severe effect on performance or stability of the bow.

RISER MATERIAL

The importance of the material used to build bow risers, or "handles" as they are referred to, has to do with the strength of that material. There are two areas in the riser where strength becomes critical.

1. It is important to make the grip section of the riser narrow or thin. If the grip area is wide it allows more hand contact and the shooter is more prone to torque the bow while shooting. The stronger the material used to build the riser, the narrower the manufacturer can design this area.

2. The vertical distance between the point where the bow hand contacts the grip and the point where the arrow rides across the arrow rest is an area of concern in riser design (figure 26). The closer these points can be located to one another, the better (less torque is introduced into the system). Stronger riser materials permit these two points to be located closer together.

Why all this concern about torque? Simply stated, torque could be described as internal

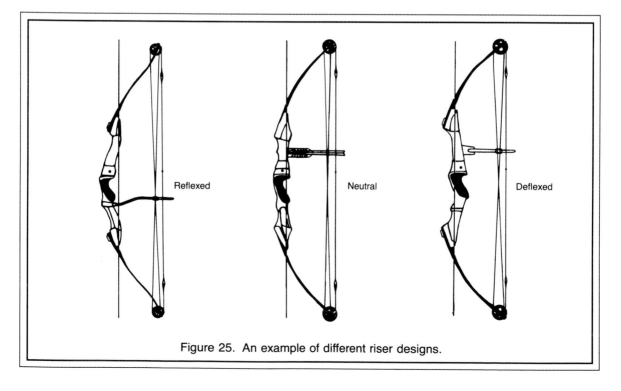

Reflexed   Neutral   Deflexed

Figure 25. An example of different riser designs.

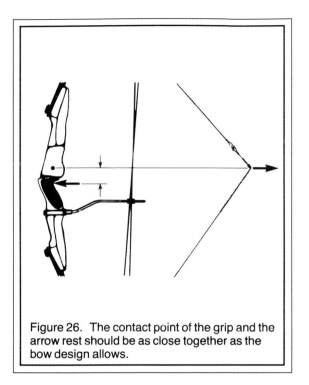

Figure 26. The contact point of the grip and the arrow rest should be as close together as the bow design allows.

twisting of the bow. When you release the string, the bow uses energy to untwist. This could cause oscillation in the arrow and wasted energy. I have consistently had better paper test (arrow flight) on bows that had less system torque.

How much does system torque affect arrow speed, arrow flight, accuracy, etc.? I honestly do not know, but I strongly prefer a bow with as little system torque as possible. System torque has absolutely no benefit.

MACHINED AND FORGED RISERS

The strongest risers are produced by machining or forging the riser from solid aluminum alloy stock. Using this material produces a riser that will withstand about 75,000 pounds per square inch (PSI). Heavy hunting bows can produce over 20,000 PSI of stress in the grip area of the riser. With this safety margin, manufacturers using solid aluminum alloy stock are

able to make the grip area of these risers narrower and to place the grip and the arrow rest closer together. This produces the best riser possible because less system torque is introduced into the bow.

Now, the bad news. Risers made from high quality solid aluminum alloy stock cost about three or four times as much to produce as risers from the other materials, and they usually weigh more. Because of the cost, most manufacturers do not offer this type of riser. This severely limits your choice of bows if you insist on a machined or forged riser.

DIE-CAST RISERS

By far, the majority of metal risers in use today are made from cast magnesium alloy, cast aluminum alloy or a combination of these materials. Risers made from these materials have a strength of about 25,000 PSI. As stated earlier, heavy hunting bows can produce over 20,000 PSI in the grip section of the riser. For this reason, the manufacturer must be sure to design the riser with enough strength to withstand that kind of stress. The only way to accomplish this with a cast riser is to leave more material in the grip area than would be necessary with a forged or machined riser made from solid aluminum alloy stock. Although manufacturers attempt to make their cast risers very strong, failures of cast risers are certainly not an unheard of occurrence.

The good news about cast risers is they are very reasonably priced and are stronger than wood. Cast risers are also lighter in weight compared to their machined counterparts. These characteristics make them the most popular type of riser available today.

WOOD RISERS

Wood is the weakest of the popular materials used to make risers. For this reason, more material must be left in the grip area of the wood riser than in a cast riser. Consequently, a wood riser bow is more likely to exhibit system torque than a metal riser bow. Again, because of strength limitations, wood risers are generally not cut as far past center as their metal counterparts.

Wood is not without its strong points. It is naturally beautiful and makes a very attractive riser. Generally, wood risers cost less to produce and a wood riser bow is much more pleasant to carry on a frosty morning.

OFF-SET RISERS

The latest choice in riser design is the off-set or dogleg. Basically, an off-set riser is one that has been cut farther past center than a normal riser (figure 27). Although not new, they have been reintroduced recently, primarily to accommodate overdraw systems. Because of strength requirements, this design has been essentially limited to metal risers. The additional off-set allows room for broadheads to be drawn back onto the overdraw without making contact with the riser. Even if you don't use an overdraw, an off-set riser offers two additional benefits:

1. It provides extra clearance for the fletching. This reduces the chances of feather or vane contact with the side of the riser when the arrow is released. Some riser designs need this additional space more than others, but in any case, a little extra doesn't hurt.
2. It allows the arrow length to be shortened by about 1 to 1½ inches without adding an overdraw because the broadhead can be drawn back almost to the arrow rest. But always use caution when choosing your arrow length; it's much better to have them a little too long.

BOW LENGTH

The length of a recurve bow is referred to in inches, such as a "60-inch" bow. The overall length of a compound bow is referred to as the "axle-to-axle" length. This is the measurement from wheel axle to wheel axle.

A bow's overall length affects the amount of finger pinch the shooter will feel from the string when drawing the bow. The longer your draw length, the more acute the angle from the limb tip to your anchor point when you are at full draw. This angle is what causes the string to pinch the fingers. Basically, the longer your draw length, the more a longer bow helps to reduce the angle and prevent finger pinch. This situation is not as critical for the release shooter because of the smaller contact point that a release has with the bow string.

Short bows are definitely more enjoyable to carry and to shoot in tight situations. On the

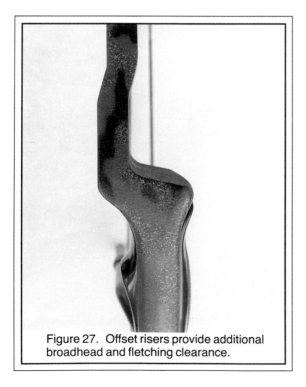

Figure 27. Offset risers provide additional broadhead and fletching clearance.

negative side, they are more critical and less stable to shoot than their longer counterparts. As mentioned above, they can also cause finger pinch. A rule of thumb is not to go too extreme in either direction. Recurve shooters should stay within 58 to 66 inches while compound shooters should stay within 42 to 48 inches.

When choosing a new bow, comfort is an important consideration. If your fingers hurt every time you shoot the bow, practicing will not be enjoyable. If you are planning to purchase a new bow, it is advisable to shoot several different bow lengths before making a final selection.

THE OVERDRAW SYSTEM

The basic benefit and purpose of an overdraw system is to facilitate the shooting of a shorter, lighter weight arrow without reducing the draw weight of the bow. Overdraws that attach to the riser, allowing the arrow rest to be moved closer to the string, are the most beneficial in terms of arrow speed because they do not reduce the power stroke of the bow. Forward handle overdraws do shorten the power stroke and consequently reduce the bow's potential for storing energy. For this reason a forward handle overdraw bow will not shoot an arrow as fast, if the other elements remain equal.

The first and most obvious way in which arrow weight is reduced is simply by shortening the arrow. Aluminum arrow shaft material weighs from 9 to 14.5 grains per inch. If an overdraw allowed you to shorten your arrow length 5 inches, that would reduce arrow weight 45 grains or more.

Whenever the arrow length is shortened, the spine (stiffness) of the arrow is increased. Because the shorter arrow will be stiffer, a smaller, lighter weight shaft can be used at the same draw weight. For example: You shoot a 70-pound bow and have a 31-inch draw length. The recommended arrow is a 2216, which would weigh about 560 grains. By shortening your arrow length by 5 inches with an overdraw system, you could theoretically shoot a 2013 arrow weighing approximately 420 grains. The total arrow weight reduction in this case would be about 140 grains, which would increase arrow speed approximately 22 FPS but reduce kinetic energy about 3½ percent. Reducing arrow weight causes both beneficial and negative effects which were covered in the chapters on "The Compound Bow at Work" and "Trajectory."

To prevent a misunderstanding here, it should be pointed out that there are often other options for reducing arrow weight that do not include adding an overdraw system. But the longer your draw length, the more difficult it becomes to reduce arrow weight and maintain sufficient spine for heavy draw weight bows. The bowhunter who insists on shooting a light arrow but has a long draw length and shoots a heavy bow, may find an overdraw the only option. Consult an Easton Aluminum arrow selection chart and the chapter on "Arrows" for details.

An overdraw is generally believed to make a bow more exacting or sensitive to shoot. Hand torque is increased because of a lever effect. See figure 28 on the next page. The lateral distance between the points where the bow hand contacts the riser (the grip) and where the arrow contacts the riser (the arrow rest) is increased dramatically with the use of an overdraw. This distance magnifies the effect of hand torque and makes the bow more difficult to shoot accurately. It should be pointed out, however, that some experts do not agree with this theory.

Finally, there are three additional points to consider if you plan to use an overdraw. First, shorter arrows are less stable in flight, espe-

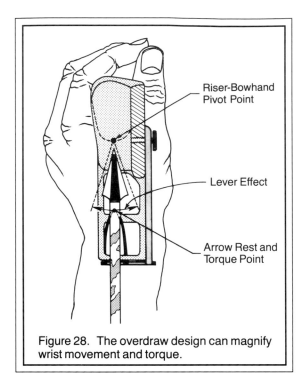

Figure 28. The overdraw design can magnify wrist movement and torque.

Riser-Bowhand Pivot Point

Lever Effect

Arrow Rest and Torque Point

the arrow. Cable guards also reduce cable vibration and noise. A negative aspect is that they add torque to the system and, by doing so, reduce performance and efficiency slightly. If you look at the cables, you can see how they pull more on the limb tips once they are placed on the cable guard.

Two steps can be taken to minimize the torque a cable guard causes:

1. Use a cable guard with a dogleg (figure 29). It doesn't matter if this type of cable guard attaches above or below the grip. It will allow the contact point with the cable to be placed closer to the center point between the limb tips. This accomplishes two things:
   a. It places a more equal amount of torque on each limb tip.
   b. It reduces the overall torque because the angle is not as acute.

cially when equipped with a broadhead. A rule of thumb is to stay above 24 inches. Second, the broadhead is drawn back behind the bowhand; this gives some shooters an uneasy feeling in regard to safety. Third, some bowhunters find that they need a release aid when shooting an overdraw system because, as mentioned above, they are reported to be more sensitive to shoot.

The bottom line is whether or not an overdraw will work for you. If you try an overdraw, keep a close eye on your accuracy. If you are willing to accept both the good and bad aspects of an overdraw system, its effect on your shooting accuracy should be the determining factor in your choice.

CABLE GUARDS

A cable guard holds the cables to the side and thus prevents contact with the fletching of

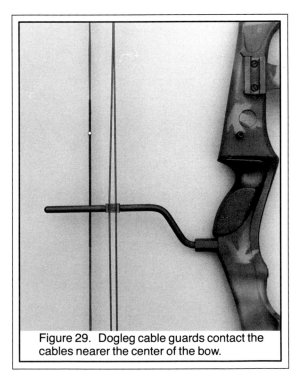

Figure 29. Dogleg cable guards contact the cables nearer the center of the bow.

2. The second step is a simple matter of making sure you do not set the cable guard out farther than necessary; however, be sure the fletching of your arrow is not contacting the cables when you release.

The cable guard can become loose and rotate, allowing the fletching of the arrow to make contact with the cables. If this happens, it can damage the cables and fletching and adversely affect arrow flight. Get in the habit of checking for rough spots in the cable coating by feeling the cables between your thumb and index finger a few inches above and below the cable guard. Also remember to remove your cables from the cable guard when storing the bow for a long period of time.

Several bow manufacturers offer wide-wheel models (cams) that they claim do not need cable guards (figure 30). All of the wide-wheel bows I have set up for friends were ultimately equipped with cable guards. The need for a cable guard on a wide-wheel bow can vary greatly from shooter to shooter for the following reasons:

1. The amount of torque in the system partly introduced by the shooter's grip.
2. Cleanness of the shooter's release.
3. Diameter of the shaft and size of fletching used on the arrow.

It is far more damaging to the bow's performance to have an arrow or fletching contact the cables than it is to push the cables out farther than necessary. Be sure that you maintain ample cable clearance without overdoing it. Check periodically for any changes and damage to the cables.

THE BOW STRING

The bow string could be considered the

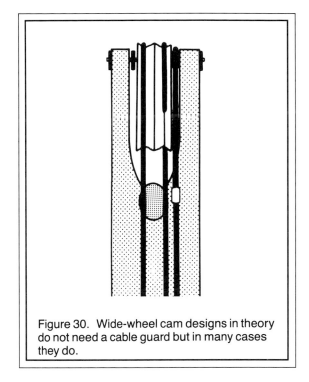

Figure 30. Wide-wheel cam designs in theory do not need a cable guard but in many cases they do.

"Rodney Dangerfield" of archery equipment. It gets no respect. But the string is one of the most fragile and yet important parts of your bow. Frankly, I am surprised by the lack of consideration given to the string by many bowhunters. The following discussion of the bow string will help you get the most from this often overlooked part of the bow.

STRING LENGTH

String length affects the draw length, draw weight and the brace height of a compound bow, which in turn can affect the bow's performance. A longer string increases the draw length, draw weight and the cable wrap on the cams, but it lowers the brace height. A shorter string has the opposite effect. The brace height is particularly important to the recurve shooter. Most recurve bows can be fine tuned by adjusting the string length.

A new string will stretch, the majority of

which will occur during the first 25 shots. The amount of stretch depends upon the draw weight of the bow and the quality and number of strands in the string. Some inexpensive strings will stretch up to ¾ inch. After changing strings, always check for cable overlap, which can be a dangerous situation (figure 31). If there is not room for the edge of a quarter between where the cables would overlap, a shorter string is recommended.

The bowstring can be shortened a little by twisting. My custom string maker recommends not to shorten the overall length of the string more than ¼ inch by twisting. Some experts recommend that the string not be twisted at all when used on a compound bow with standard cables. They believe the twist in the string can cause the untwisting of the cables. This untwisting can in turn weaken the attachment between the cable fibers and the teardrops. The bow string attaches directly to the teardrops

on most standard compound bows with cables. When a cable does fail, it is most often where the teardrop attaches to the cable fibers.

CUSTOM-MADE STRINGS

A reasonable option for changing string length in small amounts is to have a string custom made to the length needed. I can't remember owning a bow that required an even length string after being set to my exact draw length. But this isn't the only reason to choose a custom-made string. They are generally of much higher quality than the mass produced strings. Using one certainly raises my confidence level, and sometimes this is the most important consideration. A good custom string maker should be happy to make a string for you in any length necessary (within ¼ inch after stretching). A well-made custom string will cost three to five times more than a factory made string but it is worth the extra cost.

REPLACING A STRING

When hunting, you should always have an extra string available. It's easy to damage a bow string and there is no reason to take this chance. Your extra string should be set up exactly like your primary string and shot-in at least 25 times. Next, measure the length of each string while it is on the bow. The replacement strings should be within ¼ inch of the primary string. Fortunately, most compound bows come with double teardrop cables, which makes changing strings a very simple procedure.

A quick way to change strings when the bow is equipped with double teardrop cables is as follows: Stand on one foot and lift the other knee as high as possible; hook the grip of the riser just below the raised knee. For extra support, lean against a tree or wall. Now pull on the old string just enough to hook on the

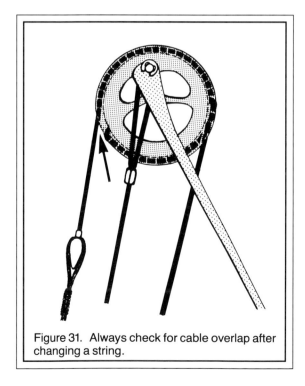

Figure 31. Always check for cable overlap after changing a string.

new string. Relax the pressure. Next pull on the new string just enough to remove the old string (figure 32). Use caution when changing a string in this manner; make sure the bow doesn't slip off your knee.

STRING CARE

Many hunters I have met in the field have bow strings that are in poor condition. These continued observations are what prompted my opening statement about the bow string getting no respect. The best protection for your bow string is wax. Proper and consistent waxing of your bow string will extend its life up to five times that of an unwaxed string. The best wax to use is the commercial type found in archery shops, but beeswax will also work. Think of a string without wax as you would an engine without oil.

When hunting on foot in rough country, I wax my string every other day. When hunting from treestands, I wax my string every three or four days. I also wax my string heavily before putting it on the bow and often while practicing. Make sure you wax the complete string, including the end loops.

Using the above procedure for the past ten years, I have never had to replace a string during a hunting season. I have used some strings for two years, changing them at that time only as a precaution.

THE NOCKING POINT

The nocking point is the location on the string at which the nock of the arrow is placed. Most of my bows seem to shoot best with the nocking point $\frac{1}{16}$- to $\frac{1}{8}$-inch above square. In other words, add $\frac{1}{16}$-inch to the diameter of the shaft size (figure 33) you are shooting and find that mark on your bow square. Remember, this is just a starting place. The nocking point location can vary considerably from bow to

Figure 32. Changing a string

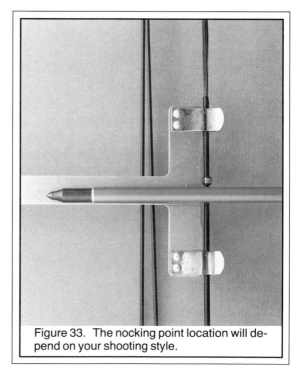

Figure 33. The nocking point location will depend on your shooting style.

bow and with your individual shooting style. After the proper nocking point is determined, a nock locator or two should be crimped in place.

The most important aspect of the nocking point, after determining its proper location, is making sure the nock locator does not move. If you are a finger shooter, I recommend at least one nock locator and a small amount of dental floss or other type of material tied directly above to ensure that it doesn't move. If you are a release shooter, I would suggest two nock locators and the dental floss to help hold them in place. There are also larger, hunter nock locators, as they are sometimes called, which were designed for the 18-strand strings. These larger nock locators will work on 16-strand strings and usually require only one nock set along with dental floss even when using a release aid.

CENTER SERVING SIZE (NOCK FIT)

How a nock fits the string may seem insignificant to some, but I find it an extremely important consideration. If the nock is too tight on the string serving, it can affect bow performance and arrow flight. A tight-fitting nock will also make a rather loud snap when going on and off the string. This noise can be critical under certain hunting conditions. If the nock fit is too loose, the arrow can fall from the string at the most inopportune time. Worse yet, the arrow could slip off when you are at full draw without your knowing it, causing a dry fire.

Three elements affect the diameter of the center serving:

1. The number of strands in the string—most hunting bow strings vary from 14 to 18; most cam bow strings have 18 strands.
2. The size of monofilament material used

for the serving—.018 and .021 are common.
3. The amount of tension used to apply the monofilament to the string directly affects the center serving size.

If my nocks do not fit a new string perfectly, I remove the old center serving and replace it with a new one, using enough tension to make the nocks fit exactly. Replacing the serving is time consuming but it ensures the best possible results. I recommend using monofilament material for the center serving because it wears better than nylon thread. This is particularly important if you shoot a release. It should be noted, however, that some bowhunters prefer nylon servings primarily because they are easier to repair in the field.

The slot in the nock can be filed out to make it accept a larger serving, but this is time consuming and a pain in the neck. In the long run, changing to a larger nock size or replacing the serving is a better idea.

Compressing a nock slightly with your teeth is a common way to make it fit more tightly on the string. This may do in an emergency but is not recommended for obvious reasons. A better temporary solution is to add a little dental floss below the nock locator where the nock contacts the string. A few wraps for about ⅜ of an inch will usually do the trick. The dental floss may last from a few days to months, depending on the amount of shooting and how well you tied the knots.

Dental floss has several other uses when it comes to archery equipment. It is a handy item to have in your tackle box. Here are some uses you should keep in mind:

This is my favorite. Tie a 4- to 6-inch length of dental floss on the top limb axle between the axle keeper and the outside of the limb. After chewing on the loose end for a while, it will become frayed, making an excellent wind detector. Seriously, I would not be without this little device. It is vital for keeping track of the wind during a stalk. The dental floss does occasionally get tangled in the upper wheel and torn off the axle. But this does not happen often and, at worst, you simply replace the floss.

Dental floss is also handy for tying off servings that get frayed or start coming loose. It can also be used to protect a frayed area of the bow string from further damage. Of course, these are only temporary solutions, but they will work in an emergency.

PEEP SIGHTS

The peep sight is a small ring which fits into the bow string and functions as a rear sight in conjunction with your pins (front sight). The hole in the peep sight is aligned with and looked through by your shooting eye (figure 34). The advantage of a peep sight is that it

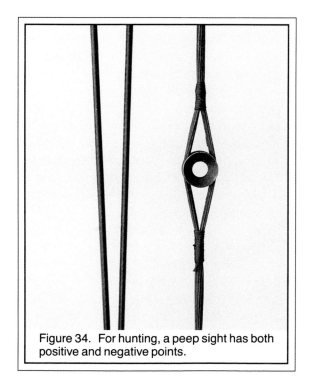

Figure 34. For hunting, a peep sight has both positive and negative points.

gives you one more check point, hence providing a more stable anchor and, consequently, better accuracy.

A disadvantage to the peep sight is that it can be difficult to see through during low-light conditions. If the bowstring is not drawn the same each time, the peep can stop sideways, blocking your vision. Fine-Line Inc. (11220 164 St. E., Puallup WA 98374) offers a self-centering peep that helps prevent this problem. The Fine-Line peep sight uses surgical tubing attached to the upper limb and the string, assuring that the peep will be positioned properly at full draw. This peep sight looks a little strange when attached to the bow, but it does work. Most peep sights take some time and patience to install correctly.

The larger the hole in the peep, the easier it is to see through, of course, but it also allows more variability in the anchor point. Hunters usually use a peep with a rather large opening for better visibility. A peep sight will help most shooters' accuracy, but many bowhunters do not like to use a peep sight. The only way to find out how much a peep sight will help your accuracy is to give one a try. Give yourself some time to become familiar with the peep sight and make sure it is tied into the string securely. I do not use a peep sight myself, but I know several hunters who use them successfully.

SILENCERS

String silencers affect the bow two ways, but only one is beneficial. See figure 35 on the next page. The benefit is that silencers absorb vibrations during the shot and thus reduce noise, giving you a quieter bow. This helps prevent animals jumping the string.

The negative effect is that silencers absorb energy that otherwise would have been delivered to the arrow. The energy lost is minute as long as the amount of silencer material is

Figure 35. Two styles of silencers.

kept in the light to moderate range.

I prefer the rubber-type silencer over the yarn-type. Some yarn-type silencers will absorb moisture in wet weather. This can make their weight vary considerably.

CHOOSING A BOW

One basic difference between the gun and bow is that a gun uses an explosive to propel its projectile while a bow uses only energy from your body. The stored energy in the bow's limbs could be compared to the gunpowder in a rifle bullet. Like the gunpowder, more is not always better. There seems to be a split among bowhunters, those in favor of heavy, slower-moving arrows and those in favor of extremely lightweight, faster-moving arrows. My personal equipment represents a blend of these two positions. As much as possible, I have tried to maintain the strong points from both

extremes. This approach has worked well for me.

Choosing a bow is truly a personal decision. More than likely, the only point upon which we could all agree is that we want the best bow for the money. Your ace in the hole when choosing equipment is knowledge. My preference for a hunting bow is a sensible compromise between the extremes in all areas. For those interested, I have listed my personal equipment choices below. The intent of this book, however, is to increase your knowledge, not to choose your equipment for you. You should use the equipment that fulfills your needs and desires.

1. Cam: My choice is a modified cam that causes the bow to store between 68 and 74 foot pounds of energy when the bow is set to AMO standards (60-pounds draw weight, 30-inch draw length). As much as possible, the modified cam should have a smooth, rounded, force-draw curve.

2. Bow efficiency: Here is the hidden plum in the pie! Why not pick the most efficient bow from the ones that offer the other choices you consider important? When considering bow efficiency, keep in mind that a bow's loss in efficiency comes in a percentage. For example, it would not be fair to compare two bows set to AMO standards if one stored 80 foot pounds of energy and the other stored 60. When comparing bows for efficiency, make sure they store a similar amount of energy or make the adjustment from the information given in the "Bow Report."

3. Bow limbs: The gap between FRP and wood laminated limbs has narrowed considerably in the past several years. But overall, I still have a strong preference for a good, wood laminated limb. This is particularly true when it comes to a com-

pound bow with working recurve limbs. The gap in efficiency between the two materials increases when both are used in a working, recurve limb design.

4. Riser: Personally, I would prefer to have a bow with a forged or machined metal alloy riser, which I consider the strongest and most dependable. A properly designed riser from this type of material would also cause the least amount of torque. Unfortunately, I have not been able to find a bow with a machined or forged riser that meets my other needs. My second choice is a cast alloy riser. For the past several years, I have used mostly bows with cast alloy risers, and they have functioned well.

Here are the other features I consider important:

1. Comfortable grip.
2. Moderate axle-to-axle length (44 to 46 inches for my 29¾-inch draw length).
3. Approximately 50-percent let-off.
4. Large sight window (The location of your anchor point determines the size of the sight window you will need). The lower your anchor, the larger the sight window requirement.
5. Camouflage.

When it comes to that final choice of bows, I have found it necessary to make compromises. In addition to the machined riser mentioned earlier, I have not been able to locate a satisfactory, modified cam on a bow meeting my other requirements. One compromise I have used is to shoot round wheel bows. I find that I can comfortably draw a few extra pounds when shooting a round wheel bow. By adding these few pounds, I gain back a little of the speed lost by not using a modified cam. Another option has been to build bows by adding a modified cam to a bow meeting my other requirements. **NOTE: This procedure is not recommended because it will void all warranties, may cause bow failure and possibly serious injury**.

Like me, you may find that you are forced to compromise when choosing a new bow. I am looking forward to the day when a manufacturer will include all points I consider important in one bow; they are coming closer all the time.

ARROWS 8

Robin Hood is best known for splitting an arrow that was already dead center in the bull's-eye of the target. So amazing was this feat that it is known to this day as a "Robin Hood." History has a way of exaggerating the truth; but, if this type of accuracy was anywhere near reality, you can rest assured Mr. Hood was a meticulous arrow maker.

An arrow's ability to fly straight and true is accomplished through careful selection and assembly of the arrow's components, as well as proper bow tuning. For the arrow to do its part properly, careful consideration and selection must be made in regard to shaft and fletching material, straightness, weight, spine (stiffness) and durability. Additionally, an arrow should have a properly aligned nock and broadhead. A final check of the completed arrow should then be made for proper balance. This chapter discusses selection and assembly of arrow components. Its purpose is to help you have the most accurate and dependable arrows possible.

SHAFT MATERIALS

For many thousands of years, wood was the primary material used for making arrow shafts. It was only within the last 50 years that other types of material were successfully used to make high-quality arrows. In 1939, Doug Easton introduced aluminum tubing as a new arrow shaft material. These newfangled shafts did not immediately dominate the market, but in time, aluminum proved itself as a lightweight, uniform shaft material. In the 1950's, fiberglass shafts were introduced and became quite popular with many archers. But the popularity and quality of aluminum shafts continued to increase. By the late 1960's, the use of fiberglass had diminished and aluminum was the shaft of choice. Today, even though arrow shafts are made from a variety of materials, there is no doubt that aluminum is king.

Before discussing today's most popular shaft materials in detail, I would like to clear up a possible misunderstanding about arrow weights and shaft sizes. When arrows are made from the same size shaft material, some bowhunters assume that completed arrows will weigh the same. While it is true that manmade shaft materials of a given size and brand start out at the same weight, the completed arrows do not necessarily weigh the same. For example, the difference between feathers and vanes could amount to more than 30 grains. The difference between broadheads could amount to 80 grains or more. The difference between inserts (carbon and aluminum) could amount to 30 grains. When one arrow's overall shaft length is longer than another's, the difference can be up to 15 grains per inch. Therefore, the finished weight of two arrows made from the same shaft size could be over 100 grains apart even when they are the same length.

ALUMINUM ALLOY SHAFTS

Aluminum alloy shaft material is certainly the most popular shaft material used today. This is true for both target competition and bowhunting. Although aluminum shaft material is more expensive than wood, aluminum shafts come from the factory matched in physical weight, straightness and spine weight. Wood shaft material does not come close to meeting these same tolerances straight from the factory. The consistency of aluminum shaft material makes completing aluminum arrows far less labor intensive. This helps balance the cost between high-quality wood and aluminum arrows. In fact, the best wood arrows are often more expensive.

The largest manufacturer of aluminum shaft material in the world today is Easton Aluminum, Inc. Easton Aluminum produces four grades of aluminum shafts for the bowhunter. They also produce a multitude of sizes and spine weights. Check with your local pro shop for a copy of "Bowhunting with Easton Aluminum Arrow Shafts." This booklet is free and contains loads of valuable information. It is a must if you wish to understand your choices of aluminum arrow shaft sizes and materials.

The selection of the correct arrow shaft size can be confusing. Much of the decision hinges on what you are trying to accomplish (i.e., penetration, increasing arrow speed or a compromise). The Easton Aluminum Hunting Shaft Selection Chart lists several shaft sizes for each draw weight and draw length category. In many cases, this selection in arrow shaft sizes will vary in physical weight by over 100 grains.

If you order arrows only by draw weight and draw length at different times or locations, you could end up with very different physical weight arrows. For example, you need arrows for an AMO bow (60 pounds draw weight and 30-inch draw length). You could choose a 2213 which weighs 485 grains or a 2020 which weighs 595 grains. Although both sizes would be properly spined for your equipment, they would not have the same point of impact or arrow speed because of the difference in physical weight. Still referring to an AMO bow (60 pound draw weight, 30-inch draw length), Easton lists a total of five acceptable arrow shaft sizes with the 551-grain 2117 being listed as the most popular choice. This information shows there is much room for personal preference.

Easton Aluminum has developed several new shaft sizes in recent years. The majority of these new arrow sizes are lighter and stiffer. Shafts are generally made lighter by increasing the diameter and reducing the wall thickness (figure 36). Easton's new arrow sizes include the 2215, 2217, 2312, 2314, 2315, 2317, 2412, 2413, 2419 and the 2512. Many of these new sizes provide more spine (stiffness) and less physical weight than any previous shafts. Reducing arrow weight flattens trajectory (see the chapter on "Trajectory"). The new shaft sizes will give bowhunters who are interested in reducing arrow weight and trajectory more

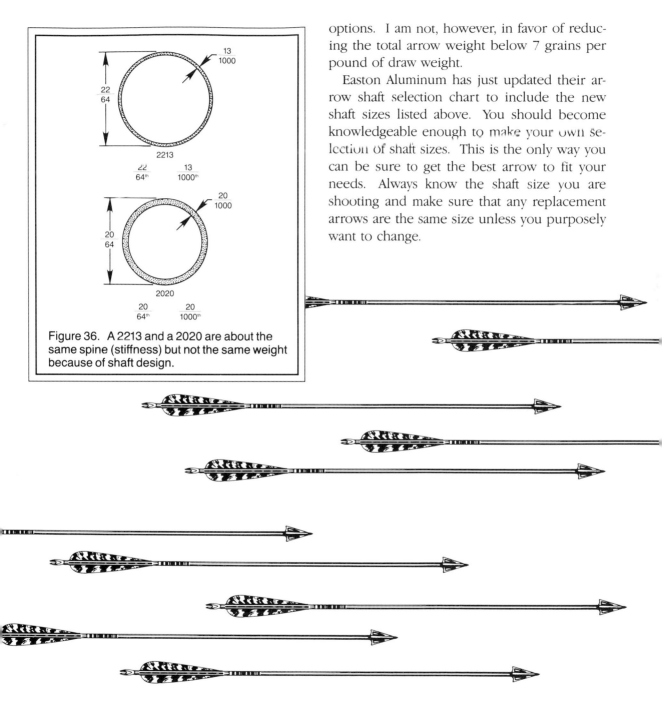

Figure 36. A 2213 and a 2020 are about the same spine (stiffness) but not the same weight because of shaft design.

options. I am not, however, in favor of reducing the total arrow weight below 7 grains per pound of draw weight.

Easton Aluminum has just updated their arrow shaft selection chart to include the new shaft sizes listed above. You should become knowledgeable enough to make your own selection of shaft sizes. This is the only way you can be sure to get the best arrow to fit your needs. Always know the shaft size you are shooting and make sure that any replacement arrows are the same size unless you purposely want to change.

To help you with your selection of aluminum arrows refer to Easton's Shaft Selection Chart on the next page.

EASTON ALUMINUM HUNTING

(Bold numbers indicate most popular size selection)

CORRECT HUNTING ARROW LENGTH
(Your Draw Length Plus 1″ Clearance)

22½–23½″		23½–24½″		24½–25½″		25½–26½″		26½–27½″		27½–28½″		28½–29½″		29½–30½″		30½–31½″		31½–32½″		32½–33½″		33½–34½″	
23″		24″		25″		26″		27″		28″		29″		30″		31″		32″		33″		34″	
Shaft Size	Arrow Weight	Shaft Size	Arrow Weight	Shaft Size	Arrow Weight	Shaft Size	Arrow Weight	Shaft Size	Arrow Weight	Shaft Size	Arrow Weight	Shaft Size	Arrow Weight	Shaft Size	Arrow Weight	Shaft Size	Arrow Weight	Shaft Size	Arrow Weight	Shaft Size	Arrow Weight	Shaft Size	Arrow Weight
		1713	223	1713	230	**1813** 1815	**251** 273	1815 **1816** 1913	282 **298** 278	1913 1915 **1916**	286 307 **332**	1818 **1916** 2013 1917	356 **342** 317 361	1917 1918 **2016** 2114	372 396 **371** 354	1918 2016 **2114** 2115	407 382 **364** 392	**2115** 2018 2213	**402** 446 378	2213 2312 2215 **2117**	388 401 415 **455**	**2215** 2314	**426** 443
1713	215	1713	223	**1813** 1815	**243** 264	1815 **1816** 1913	273 **289** 269	1913 1915 **1916**	278 298 **322**	1818 **1916** 2013 1917	346 **332** 308 351	1917 1918 **2016** 2114	361 384 **361** 344	1918 2016 2114 2115	396 371 354 381	2018 **2115** 2213	433 **392** 368	2312 2215 2020 2215 **2117**	391 415 483 405 **443**	2314 **2216** 2413 2217	432 **459** 429 481	**2314** 2413	**443** 439
1713	215	**1813** 1815	**235** 256	1815 **1816** 1913	264 **279** 261	1913 1915 **1916**	269 289 **312**	1818 **1916** 2013 1917	335 **322** 299 340	1917 1918 **2016** 2114	351 373 **350** 334	1918 2016 **2114** 2115	384 361 **344** 370	2018 **2115** 2213	421 **381** 358	2213 2312 2215 **2117** 2314 2216	368 382 394 **431** 411 447	2312 2020 2215 2314 **2216**	382 470 405 422 **447**	2314 2216 2413 **2315** 2219	432 459 429 **467** 481	2413 **2315** 2219	439 **479** 529
1813 1815	**227** 247	1815 **1816** 1913	256 **270** 253	1913 1915 **1916**	261 280 **302**	1818 **1916** 2013 1917	324 **312** 290 329	1917 1918 **2016** 2114 2115	340 361 **340** 334 359	2018 **2115** 2213	409 **370** 349	2213 2312 2020 2215 **2117**	358 372 456 383 **419**	2215 2020 2215 2117 2314 **2216**	383 470 405 419 422 **435**	2314 2413 2217 **2315** 2219	411 418 468 **467** 515	2413 **2216** 2217 2315 2219	429 **459** 481 467 515	2413 **2315** 2219	439 **479** 529
1815 **1816** 1913	247 **261** 244	1913 1915 **1916**	253 271 **292**	1818 **1916** 2013 1917	314 **302** 281 318	1917 1918 **2016** 2114 2115	329 350 **329** 315 349	1918 2016 **2114** 2115	361 340 **325** 349	2213 2312 2215 **2117**	349 363 373 **407**	2018 2020 2215 2117 2314 **2216**	443 443 373 407 390 **411**	2020 2215 2117 2314 2413 **2315**	456 405 419 400 398 **444**	2216 2413 2217 **2315** 2219	435 408 456 **456** 501	2413 2217 **2315** 2219	418 468 **467** 515	2219 2512 **2317**	529 447 **533**
1913 1915 **1916**	244 262 **282**	1818 **1916** 2013 1917	303 **292** 272 308	1917 1918 **2016** 2114	318 338 **318** 305	1918 2016 **2114** 2115	350 329 **315** 338	2018 **2115** 2213	384 **349** 329	2213 2312 2020 2215 2117 **2314** 2216	339 354 429 362 395 **379** 399	2020 2215 2413 2217 **2315** 2219	429 362 387 430 **409** 446	2314 2413 2217 **2315** 2219	390 398 443 **432** 474	2413 2217 **2315** 2219	408 456 **456** 487	2512 **2317**	437 **520**	2512 **2317**	447 **533**
1916 2013	**282** 263	1917 1918 **2016** 2114	308 326 **308** 295	1918 **2016** 2114 2115	338 318 **305** 327	2018 **2115** 2213	372 **338** 319	2213 2312 2020 2215 **2117** 2314 2216	329 344 416 351 **383** 368 387	2312 2020 2215 2117 2314 **2216**	363 416 362 395 379 **399**	2314 2216 2413 2217 **2315** 2219	390 411 398 443 **432** 474	2216 2413 2217 **2315** 2219	423 408 456 **444** 487	2512 **2317** 2419	416 **494** 519	2512 **2317**	437 **520**	2512 **2317**	447 **533**
2016 2114	**297** 285	1918 2016 **2114** 2115	326 308 **295** 316	2018 **2115** 2213	360 **327** 309	2213 2312 2215 2117 2314 **2216**	319 335 341 371 358 **375**	2312 2020 2215 2117 2314 **2216**	344 416 351 383 366 **387**	2216 2413 2217 **2315** 2219	399 377 418 **409** 446	2413 2217 **2315** 2219	387 430 **421** 460	2413 2217 **2315** 2219	408 456 **432** 487	2512 **2317**	416 **507**	2512 **2317**	437 **520**	2419	577
2016 **2114** 2115	297 **285** 306	2018 **2115** 2213	347 **316** 299	2213 2312 2215 **2117**	309 325 330 **359**	2312 2020 2215 2117 2314 **2216**	335 402 341 371 358 **375**	2314 2020 **2216** 2413 2217	368 402 **387** 366 405	2216 2413 2217 **2315** 2219	399 377 418 **409** 446	2413 2217 **2315** 2219	387 430 **409** 446	2219 2512 **2317**	474 406 **480**	2512 **2317**	416 **494**	2512 **2317**	427 **507**	2419	577
2115 2213	**306** 290	2213 **2216** 2117 2314 2216	299 **363** 347 336 351	2312 **2216** 2117 2314 2216	325 **363** 359 347 363	2314 **2216** 2413 2217	358 **375** 356 392	2216 2413 2217 **2315** 2219	387 366 405 **397** 432	2413 2217 **2315** 2219	377 418 **409** 446	2219 2512 2512 **2317**	460 396 406 **467**	2512 **2317**	406 **480**	2512 **2317**	416 **494**	2419	548	2419	562	2419	577
2213 2312 **2215**	290 307 **309**	2312 2215 2117 2314 **2216**	316 319 347 336 **351**	2314 **2216** 2117 2314 2216	347 **363** 346 336 351	2216 2413 2217 **2315** 2219	375 356 392 **386** 419	2216 2413 2217 **2315** 2219	387 366 405 **397** 432	2413 2217 **2315** 2219	366 405 **397** 454	2219 2512 **2317**	446 386 **454**	2512 **2317**	396 **467**	2512 **2317**	406 **480**	2419	533	2419	548	2419	562
2312 2215 2314 **2216**	307 309 326 **339**	2314 **2216** 2413 2217	336 **351** 346 367	2216 2413 2217 **2315**	363 346 380 374	2413 2217 **2315** 2219	356 392 **386** 419	2219 2512 **2317**	432 375 **441**	2219 **2317**	432 **454**	2512 **2317**	386 **467**	2419	519	2419	533	2419	548				

SHAFT SELECTION CHART

(90–110 Grains) 100 Grain Field-Point/Broadhead		(115–135 Grains) 125 Grain Field-Point/Broadhead		(140–160 Grains) 150 Grain Field-Point/Broadhead		(165–185 Grains) 175 Grain Field-Point/Broadhead	
Compound Bow Peak Weight (50% Let-off)	Actual Bow Weight (Recurve Bow)	Compound Bow Peak Weight (50% Let-off)	Actual Bow Weight (Recurve Bow)	Compound Bow Peak Weight (50% Let-off)	Actual Bow Weight (Recurve Bow)	Compound Bow Peak Weight (50% Let-off)	Actual Bow Weight (Recurve Bow)
46–51	39–43	42–47	35–39	38–43	31–35	34–39	27–31
52–57	44–48	48–53	40–44	44–49	36–40	40–45	32–36
58–63	49–53	54–59	45–49	50–55	41–45	46–51	37–41
64–69	54–58	60–65	50–54	56–61	46–50	52–57	42–46
70–75	59–63	66–71	55–59	62–67	51–55	58–63	47–51
76–81	64–68	72–77	60–64	68–73	56–60	64–69	52–56
82–87	69–73	78–83	65–69	74–79	61–65	70–75	57–61
88–93	74–78	84–89	70–74	80–85	66–70	76–81	62–66
94–99	79–83	90–95	75–79	86–91	71–75	82–87	67–71
100–105	84–88	96–101	80–84	92–97	76–80	88–93	72–76
106–111	89–93	102–107	85–89	98–103	81–85	94–99	77–81
112–117	94–98	108–113	90–94	104–109	86–90	100–105	82–86

The arrow weight in grains (437.5 grains per ounce) includes hunting R.P.S. insert weight and 35 grains (average between plastic vanes and feathers) for nock and fletching. Point weight must also be included when determining "total arrow weight." The arrow sizes shown in each box are listed according to spine from the weakest spine to the stiffest spine.

The new string materials such as Fast Flight, are lighter and stretch less; they therefore impart more energy on the arrow. Such materials may require a stiffer spine arrow. When using these materials, *strict* attention should be paid to manufacturer's recommended usage as some compound bow warranties may be voided by using non-stretch string material such as Fast Flight.

NOTE: The shaft sizes 1713 through 2512 are contractions of actual physical dimensions of the tubes-example: 2016 has a 20/64″ wall thickness.

The chart indicates that one shaft size may shoot well from your bow. The shaft size in the bold numbers is the most widely used, but you may decide to shoot a lighter shaft for flatter trajectory, or a heavier shaft for greater penetration. Also, large variations in bow efficiency, bow design, shooting style, and release may require special bow tuning or a shaft size change to accommodate these variations.

This chart reproduced by permission from Easton Aluminum.

WOOD SHAFTS

Wood is an excellent shaft material. I use wood arrows for stump shooting and small game hunting. Wood shaft material is the least expensive, at least in regard to the initial cost. Depending on the quality, wood arrows can be expensive or labor intensive if you make your own.

If you want wood arrows to approach the quality of aluminum arrows in all regards, as I do, first you must sort the shafts for straightness. You will be forced to discard or straighten about 90 percent of them. You must also weigh and spine each shaft if you want them to be matched. The shaft must also be tapered for nocks and points. After going to this much effort, it would be foolish not to dip or treat the wood in some way to help preserve the shafts.

A misconception which has generally been accepted by the archery community is that wood arrows are too weak to be used in compound bows. All arrows must have the proper spine for your draw weight and draw length, regardless of the shaft material. But I have shot wood shafts from 75-pound compound bows for 15 years and never experienced a problem. One reason wood arrows are not stressed any more by a compound bow than they are by a recurve bow is that compound bows have a reduced holding weight. When you release your fingers from the string of a 70-pound compound bow, you are actually releasing 30 to 40 pounds of draw weight. By the time the shaft is hit with the peak draw force, the arrow is already moving, something akin to moving your hand rearward to catch a hard-thrown baseball to reduce the sting.

On the other hand, the 70-pound recurve hits the motionless shaft with the full draw weight the instant you release your fingers from the string. Easton's arrow chart indicates that a compound bow requires a lighter spined arrow shaft than does a recurve bow of equal draw weight and draw length. This pattern will hold true regardless of the shaft material used to construct the arrow.

In most cases, it is true that the compound bow will deliver more energy to the arrow than a recurve bow of equal draw weight, but it does so in a different fashion. Please do not construe this information to mean that wood arrows are 100 percent safe to shoot. Because of the nature of wood, you should continually check the shafts for any cracks or weak spots as a precaution. A wood shaft could break and injure the shooter. I do feel, however, that this is no more likely to happen with a compound bow than it is with a recurve or long bow.

FIBERGLASS SHAFTS

Fiberglass arrows are very durable. They are also among the heaviest. A fiberglass arrow must be made perfectly straight the first time. Once it is made, any defect in straightness cannot be corrected. For this reason, it has been difficult to obtain acceptable fiberglass shaft material. Aluminum arrows can be straightened throughout the manufacturing process and by the consumer. This is an important luxury the fiberglass manufacturer does not have. To my knowledge, there are no fiberglass arrows being produced at this time, except for solid fiberglass fish arrows.

GRAPHITE SHAFTS

Graphite composite arrows are very light and durable, but graphite composite shaft manufacturers have faced the same problems as the fiberglass shaft manufacturers. Because of quality-control problems and cost, graphite composite shafts were never very popular and they slowly faded from the marketplace. But recently, graphite composite shafts have been reintroduced.

Of all shaft materials available, graphite has always offered the highest spine for the least amount of physical weight. If, this time, manufacturers can overcome quality-control problems, these shafts could be just the ticket for bowhunters trying to reduce arrow weight without using an overdraw. It is predictable, however, that the price will remain higher than for the other materials listed. I have not had the opportunity to test the new composite graphite shafts as of this writing.

THE NOCK

The nock must be aligned perfectly with the shaft to obtain maximum accuracy from the arrow. This makes sense because the nock is located where the string literally propels the arrow forward. I have found arrows to be more sensitive to improper nock alignment than to a slight bend in shaft material. Tests have shown that a misaligned nock can have a serious effect on the arrow's accuracy. More bad news is that a misaligned nock is more difficult to notice than a misaligned point.

One test for a misaligned nock is as follows: Rest the arrow shaft on the fingernails of the thumb and middle finger of your left hand (figure 37). With a target point in the shaft, put the point end of the arrow in the palm of the right hand. Now blow against the fletching and observe the nock as the shaft rotates. If the nock is straight, you will not see any wobble. You will feel a little silly at first and it will not be easy, but you will catch on quickly. This method of spinning the arrow can also be used to check the shaft for straightness. A handy tool specifically designed to help you find a misaligned nock is the Bjorn Nock Alignment Jig offered by Hoyt/Easton Archery Co. (605 No. Challenger Road, Salt Lake City, UT 84116-1470). Most arrow straighteners can also be used to find misaligned nocks.

Figure 37. Blowing on the fletching is one quick way to check for a misaligned nock.

Another way to test nock alignment, and the complete arrow for that matter, is to shoot each arrow. The effectiveness of this test is related directly to your personal shooting ability. The more accurately you shoot, the more obvious an arrow with any type of problem becomes. While shooting, mark all arrows that strike outside your normal group area. If an arrow consistently strikes at the edge or outside of this area, check it first for point alignment and shaft straightness. If you find nothing wrong, change the nock and test the arrow again. A word of caution when marking a suspected problem arrow, place the mark so it will not be detected when you retest the arrow. The knowledge that something is possibly wrong with a particular arrow prevents many shooters from continuing with a fair test.

To provide maximum clearance for the fletching as it passes through the arrow rest area, the nocks can be removed and new nocks relocated. After placing an arrow on the string, look through the rest area from just behind the nocking point. Observe whether a slight rotation of the fletching in either direction would provide more clearance as the arrow moves over the rest. This clearance factor becomes even more important if you shoot vanes. If you make your own arrows, consider not gluing on your nocks until after your arrows are fletched. This allows you to reposition the nock with minimal effort. By forcing the nock on without glue, it will remain secure enough to permit you to fletch the shaft. Afterward, the nock can be permanently attached in the correct location.

You should not cut nocks from the shaft with a knife. Most archers are guilty of this, including yours truly. But cutting off a nock with a knife can put flat spots on the nock swage (taper). This could cause the replacement nock to be misaligned.

The recommended method for removing nocks is to heat them over a flame and then remove the melting nock with a pair of pliers. Once the shaft has cooled, clean the nock taper with a solvent.

Nocks should also fit the string exactly—not too tight or too loose. See the chapter on "The Bow and String" (serving size).

FLETCHING MATERIAL

Fletching helps give the arrow control while in flight. The position, type and amount of fletching material on the shaft determines the amount of control it provides. The three most popular positions in which to attach fletching materials are:

1. Straight fletch is positioned straight along or parallel with the shaft (figure 38 A).
2. Straight fletch with an off-set, sometimes called spiral fletch, is positioned in a

straight line but is attached to the shaft on a slight angle (figure 38 B).
3. Helical fletch is positioned on the shaft with a clamp that imparts a slight twist or turn in the fletching material (figure 38 C).

Both the straight off-set and the helical fletch cause the shaft to rotate or spin in the air, giving the arrow more control compared to an equal amount of straight fletch. As a general rule, helical fletch offers the most control and is suggested for those using large broadheads.

FEATHERS

If we compare two shafts of the same size, one fletched with feathers and the other with an equal amount of plastic material (vanes), the feathers will provide the most control. This is because the surface area of the feather is rougher and causes more resistance or drag when moving through the air. Feathers are also softer and more forgiving. For example, the flight of a feathered arrow would not be as severely affected as the flight of a vaned arrow if both had an equal amount of contact with the arrow rest or other objects. This can be important when shooting only one arrow under cold, stressful conditions or from an awkward position.

You may have some concerns about the care of feathers in wet weather. The treatments we used many years ago did more damage than good in the long run. My preference is to start with high-quality feathers. Excellent feathers are available from Trueflight Mfg. Co., Inc. (Manitowish Waters, WI 54545). In wet weather, all I do is attach a light, plastic sandwich bag to each arrow with a small rubber band. The bags can be removed quickly from the arrows in an emergency. Depending on the hunting situation, I leave one or two arrows unbagged. If the arrows that are uncovered get too soaked, I take a break and exchange them for dry ones.

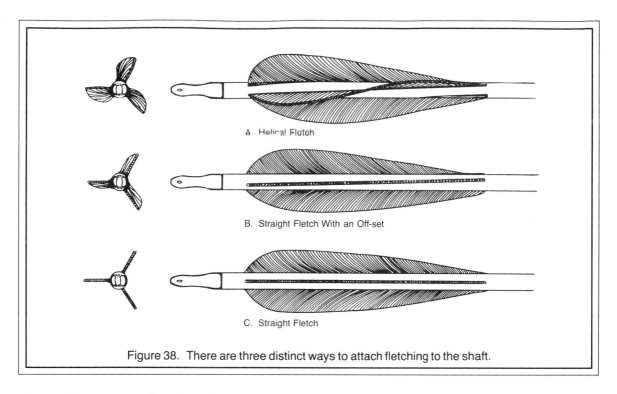

A Helical Fletch

B. Straight Fletch With an Off-set

C. Straight Fletch

Figure 38. There are three distinct ways to attach fletching to the shaft.

If you do not care for this idea, there are waterproofing materials available specifically for feathers.

A popular way to put some life back into weather-abused feathers is to steam them. This is done by boiling water in a tea kettle and rotating the feathers through the steam. Don't overdo the steam, and make sure the feathers are not touching anything while you give them plenty of time to dry.

VANES

Vanes are more durable under general shooting conditions and withstand wet hunting conditions much better than feathers. They also cause less noise if they contact brush during a stalk.

The arrow speed difference between feathers and vanes is an interesting comparison but is not as straightforward as one might think. Vanes weigh more, causing the vane-fletched arrow

to start out slower. A feathered arrow starts out faster because the feathers weigh less (by about 30 grains), but they cause more resistance while moving through the air. Because of these facts, a vaned arrow will overtake a feathered arrow between 25 and 40 yards down range, depending on the weight of the vanes. See figure 39 on the next page. From this point on, the vaned arrow is aerodynamically superior. But in my opinion, there is not enough difference between feathers and vanes regarding arrow speed to make this a consideration when choosing the type of fletching material to be used on hunting arrows.

INSERTS

Recently, Easton Aluminum has introduced carbon composite inserts. These new inserts offer two benefits. First, they weigh much less than their aluminum counterparts. This allows

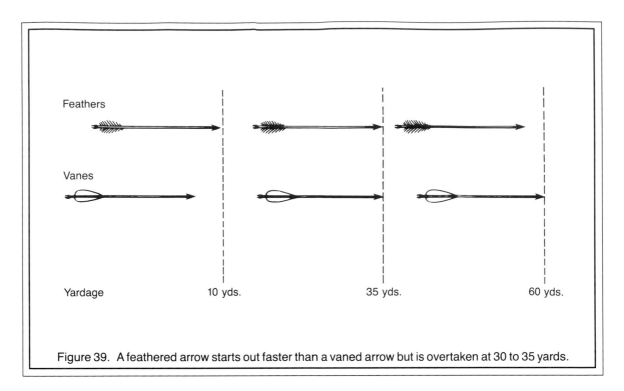

Feathers

Vanes

Yardage   10 yds.   35 yds.   60 yds.

Figure 39. A feathered arrow starts out faster than a vaned arrow but is overtaken at 30 to 35 yards.

you to reduce the overall arrow weight or put that weight into the meat of the broadhead where it will have more benefit. For example, an aluminum insert for the ever popular 2216 weighs 28 grains, while the new carbon inserts weigh only 16 grains. The same comparison for a 2413 shaft is 51 and 17 grains, respectively.

The second benefit is that the threads of the insert and screw-in points don't bind or lock together. I'm sure some of you have experienced how frustrating this seemingly minor inconvenience can be. The arrowhead is also less likely to come loose while shooting.

THE ARROWHEAD

As the weight of an arrowhead increases so does its mass, and this mass affects the spine of the shaft. This occurs because the nock end of the arrow is struck with a tremendous amount of energy when the bow string is released. The

principle of inertia dictates that the mass concentrated at the point end of the arrow shaft resist the force coming from the bow string. These opposing forces cause the shaft to flex (figure 40). As the arrowhead mass increases so does the need for a stiffer (greater spine) shaft. Easton Aluminum's latest hunting shaft selection chart adjusts the recommended arrow shaft spine according to the arrowhead weight. In addition to the effects of its weight, a broadhead's blades compete with the fletching for control of the arrow. For more information see the chapter on "Broadheads."

ARROW BALANCE

An arrowhead's weight also affects the balance of the arrow. If the completed arrow does not have enough weight at the point end of the shaft, it will not fly properly. This is usually referred to as an out-of-balance arrow. Because

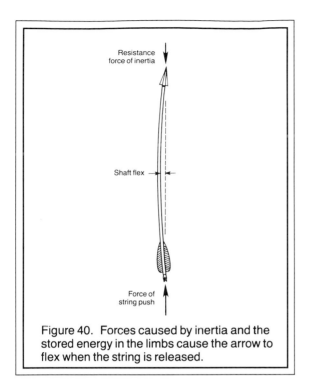

Resistance
force of inertia

Shaft flex

Force of
string push

Figure 40. Forces caused by inertia and the stored energy in the limbs cause the arrow to flex when the string is released.

most broadheads weigh 125 grains or more, and the insert usually weighs 25 grains or more, it is rare to find an out-of-balance hunting arrow. This situation is more likely to occur if you shoot arrows with vanes, long shafts and light broadheads.

The factors that affect the balance point of the arrow are the weight of the fletching, length and weight of the arrow shaft, and weight of the insert and broadhead combined. Since vanes weigh considerably more than feathers, they also change the balance point of the arrow. A longer shaft changes the balance point because it places the opposite weights at a greater separation distance, thus magnifying the effect of the difference. The weights of the broadhead and insert change the balance point because they amount to a high percentage of the arrow's weight concentrated in one location. The shaft size also changes the balance point because the weight per inch of the shaft changes

as the size changes. Regardless of the shaft size, the idea is to balance your arrows.

If you do have out-of-balance arrows, it can lead to an extremely frustrating situation. Most bowhunters would think either their bow was out of tune or they had a bad release, never thinking to check the arrows for balance.

Too much weight in the front portion of the arrow also has a negative effect, but it is not critical. The only negative effect from this situation is that the arrow will fall or die off faster after reaching the apex of its trajectory path.

The easiest way I have found to check arrows for balance is to use the following method:

1. Measure the arrow from the bottom of the nock slot to the insert. See figure 41 on the next page. Do not include the point in this measurement. Make this measurement in 16ths of an inch. For example, a 30½-inch arrow equals 488-16ths. With a calculator find 40 percent of the total arrow shaft length (i.e., 488 x 40 percent = 195). Record this number and keep it handy.

2. Next find the balance point of a complete arrow—the way you intend to use it for hunting. To do so, lay an arrow on a thin, flat object like the flat side of a narrow butter knife (anything flat, ¼ inch or so wide). Move the arrow back and forth until it is balanced. Pick the arrow up with your thumb and index finger, making sure to place your thumbnail exactly on the balance point. Place a small mark on the shaft at your thumbnail with a magic marker.

3. Now, measure the shaft material from the insert, back to the balance point. Reduce this figure to 16ths in the manner shown in the above example. If, in this case, the number is less than 195, there is no

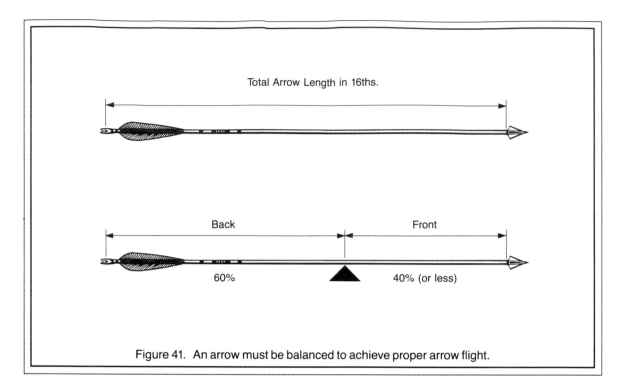

Total Arrow Length in 16ths.

Back   Front

60%   40% (or less)

Figure 41. An arrow must be balanced to achieve proper arrow flight.

problem with the example arrow. The numbers for your arrow will be different. What you should be concerned with is the percentages.

Remember that the critical situation arises when there is too little weight in the front portion of the arrow. Do not allow the balance point to fall below a 60-40 percent ratio. In other words, **not more than 40 percent of the arrow's total shaft length should be on the arrowhead end of the balance point**.

Again, the 60-40 percent ratio is the ideal figure. If the balance point is less than 40 percent toward the arrowhead side of the shaft, this is acceptable. It would only cause a slight increase in the trajectory path after the apex.

NO EXCUSES

We have all heard the horror stories about the hunter who had his feathers promptly removed from his arrows by an afternoon shower. When and if this does happen, the manufacturer or person fletching those arrows has failed miserably. There is absolutely no excuse for feathers or vanes to fall off. Ensuring that my feathers stay on is just one of the reasons I make my own arrows.

The following is a true story about one of my arrows, and it serves to better illustrate this point. Several years ago, while hunting from a favorite treestand, I shot a small bull elk. Shortly before finding the bull, I found the rear quarter of the arrow that had struck the bull behind the front shoulder. I always remove any broken arrows from the forest, so I picked up the broken portion of the arrow, moved on a short distance and found the bull. Before packing out the elk quarters, I removed my treestand and must have dropped the broken arrow at the base of the tree.

The next fall, I returned to place my stand in the same tree from which I had hunted the previous season. There in the mud, a few yards from the tree, was the feathered portion of the arrow I had used on the bull a year earlier. After chastising myself for being so careless, I became curious. So I washed the feathers in clean water and allowed them to dry. They were in very shootable condition. In fact, to remove the feathers, I had to cut them from the shaft.

When applied properly, feathers or vanes will stay on the shaft until they completely wear out or are shot off. Anything less is unacceptable. If you purchase ready-made arrows, you should take the extra time necessary to place a small amount of compatible glue at both ends and along one side of each feather or vane (figure 42). This precaution will not totally repair a poor fletching job, but it will provide extra insurance for the borderline cases.

Personally, I prefer feathers over vanes. The primary reasons for this are that feathers offer more control, weigh less and are more forgiving to contact with the rest. Another reason for my preference is that I don't like plastic fletch on my arrows. Don't ask me to justify that state-

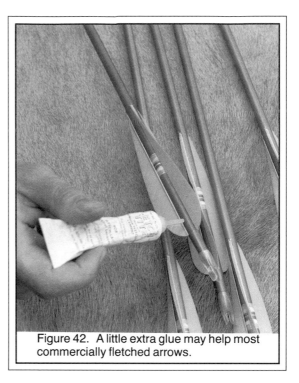

Figure 42. A little extra glue may help most commercially fletched arrows.

ment; I can't. But often it just comes down to what we like. Both feathers and vanes have their strong and weak points. Your personal choice should be based on the points you consider most important.

BROADHEADS 9

The effectiveness of today's broadhead has changed very little from that of broadheads used by our counterparts thousands of years ago. The techniques for making razor-sharp broadheads have been available since the Stone Age, and in fact were developed well ahead of the bow itself. Several types of stones were first shaped (chipped) into heads for spears. Later, these same techniques were used to make smaller points for arrows, the first broadheads. Flint and obsidian are the best known materials used to make razor-sharp stone broadheads. Several modern-day bowhunters have used stone heads to harvest big game animals. They report them to be extremely effective but somewhat fragile. When compared to the advances made in other archery equipment, the change in the *effectiveness* of the broadhead has been insignificant. There have, however, been tremendous improvements in uniformity, weight reduction, convenience and durability.

Two styles of broadheads dominate the market today: the traditional style and the replacement blade type. A tremendous number of variations are available for each style, and in recent years, there has been some blending of the two styles by various manufacturers.

TRADITIONAL STYLE BROADHEADS

The traditional broadhead is one that has a blade-type point. See figure 43 on the next page. They are known for their penetrating ability. Although penetration is something that is very difficult to measure, relative to big game animals, it is generally agreed that the traditional style broadheads do have superior penetrating capabilities. This is because a blade-type point begins to cut immediately upon contact with the target. On the negative side, the traditional broadheads do have a reputation for having slightly more flight control problems.

Most traditional style broadheads must be hand sharpened by the bowhunter. Some models are simple to sharpen, others are diffi-

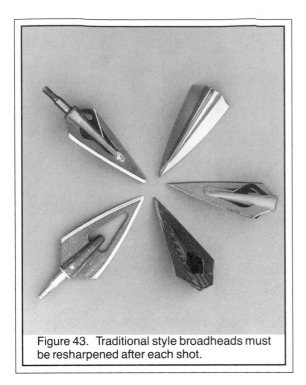

Figure 43. Traditional style broadheads must be resharpened after each shot.

that usually attach to a bullet type point (figure 44). They are known for their accuracy and convenience and for shooting in the same place as field points (they don't always). Another claim to fame is that they come from the factory razor-sharp (again they don't always). The idea behind replacement style broadheads is to replace the dull blades after each shot. Regardless of the claims by the manufacturer, all broadheads, including the replacement blade type, must be double-checked for sharpness before being used for hunting.

Many bowhunters have two misunderstandings about replacement style broadheads. First, many bowhunters believe their broadheads will stay sharp until they are shot. This is simply not true. It depends to a large degree on how they are treated. Consider how quickly your razor blade becomes dull while shaving. Broadheads will not stay sharp forever; they may be put in and taken out of your quiver

cult. One reason some heads are more difficult to sharpen than others is the number of fixed blades. When there are more than two fixed blades, they have a tendency to get in the way as you attempt to sharpen the head. The hardness of the metal is also a factor in the sharpening difficulties of broadheads. A broadhead's hardness rating should be between 44 and 48 when measured by the Rockwell system.

There are several helpful sharpening devices on the market for most models and styles of broadheads. Among the best are: Truangle Hones (R. R. # 3, Wabash, IN 46992) and Custom-Edge Broadhead Sharpeners (1616 S. Quintero Way, Aurora, CO 80017).

REPLACEMENT STYLE BROADHEADS

The replacement blade style broadhead is one that has presharpened replaceable blades

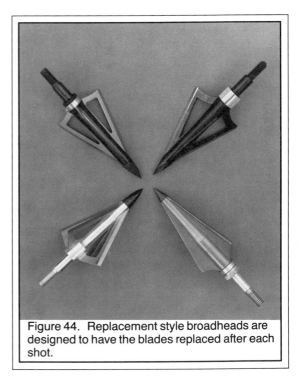

Figure 44. Replacement style broadheads are designed to have the blades replaced after each shot.

several times or even carried around loose in an arrow box.

Even broadheads left in the quiver will lose their razor-sharp edge over time. Constantly check your broadheads and touch them up or replace the blades if they have lost that razor-sharp edge. I always check my number one broadhead (the one constantly taken in and out of my quiver while hunting) to make sure the blades stay sharp.

Second, many bowhunters do not realize that replacement blade broadheads can be resharpened. In fact, the blades can be resharpened quite easily. I prefer a small steel for the job. Sharpen half of the blade, then turn it around and do the other half (figure 45). You can save money by learning to resharpen these blades. After shooting at an animal, I find that, on the average, 75 percent of the blades can be resharpened to razor-sharp condition. This average will stay constant whether you harvest or

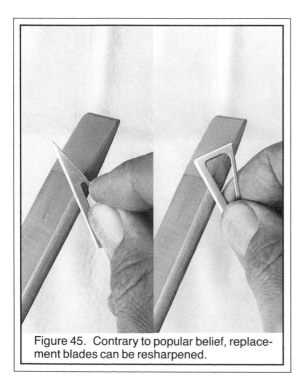

Figure 45. Contrary to popular belief, replacement blades can be resharpened.

miss the animal. Beyond the monetary aspect, there is a certain satisfaction in sharpening your own broadheads which many bowhunters miss in the name of convenience.

To deal with the problem of storing the extra blades, I have found a simple method. Use two empty plastic film canisters. Mark one "dull" and one "resharpened." Keep the dull blades in their container until you have the opportunity to resharpen them. A cotton ball and a few drops of oil placed in the container with the resharpened blades will help preserve their condition. The oil prevents the blades from rusting. The cotton ball keeps them stabilized so they do not rub together and lose their razor-sharp edge. I reuse the blades that can be satisfactorily resharpened and save the others for practice arrows. On several occasions, I have given other bowhunters dull blades when they were about to ruin new ones for practice.

BROADHEAD SIZE

Most popular broadheads range in cutting width from 1 to 1½ inches and have from two to six blades. Two, three and four blades are the most popular. A principle that should be understood regarding broadhead size is that a small three-blade head of the same length has more cutting surface than a larger two-blade head. This rule holds true when comparing a wide three-blade with a narrower four-blade broadhead.

Many bowhunters believe that a large broadhead is the key to producing a good bloodtrail. We all want a bloodtrail that is easy to follow, but is a large broadhead the answer? To prove conclusively one way or the other, it would be necessary to compare hundreds of bloodtrails caused by both large and small broadheads. After many years of keen interest in this subject, my observations have not shown this to be true. A well-defined bloodtrail appears to have more to do with the location of the wound than the size of the broadhead.

If you shoot a large broadhead and miss the vital area by 4 inches because of arrow flight problems caused by a large broadhead, what have you gained? Some bowhunters shoot the largest broadhead made, thinking this is the most important factor in harvesting a game animal. By doing so, they give up some of their potential accuracy and penetration. If, on the other hand, you can shoot a large head that does not adversely affect accuracy, trajectory or penetration, maybe you are ahead of the game.

An early hunting experience influenced my feelings concerning large broadheads, good arrow flight and overall accuracy. Shortly after moving to Colorado in the mid '60s, I felt the need to change to larger broadheads because of the opportunity to hunt elk, which are known for being tough to put down. One

afternoon, near Steamboat Springs, I shot at a magnificent four-point mule deer from a mere 20 yards. I remember the flight path of that arrow as though it were yesterday. It was headed straight for the buck's chest but, at the last instant, it took a hard left and completely missed the buck. The arrow didn't hit anything, it just turned as though it had a mind of its own. I was disappointed, devastated and confused by what had happened.

Back at camp, I shot for an hour. Some shots were fine, others seemed to float or turn for no reason. I remember blaming my release and the spine of the arrow shaft. It turned out to be neither. Looking back, the answers appear obvious. But at the time, I didn't know where or how to find those answers. It took me two years to find out that my arrows were windplaning and that the large broadheads were the significant cause. In addition, the heads were not all properly aligned, which was

most certainly a contributing factor.

A poor-flying, inaccurate, large broadhead is not as effective as an accurate, clean-flying small or medium-sized head. Again, there is nothing wrong with shooting a large broadhead if it does not affect your accuracy or arrow flight. A good accuracy test is as follows.

You will need a pencil, paper, three arrows with field points, three arrows with broadheads, and a good broadhead target. From your maximum effective range (see the chapter on "Shooting Ability"), after a few warm up shots, shoot all six arrows, alternating broadheads and field points for each shot. For this test, do not concern yourself with sight adjustment as long as both arrow types are hitting safely within the target.

Before pulling the arrows from the target, measure the group size for each arrow type. Be sure not to allow an arrow of the other type to interfere with your measurement. Record your findings in separate columns in this form: 10.3 inches for field points, 11.8 inches for broadheads, and so on. Shoot all six arrows at least five times each. When you have completed your shooting, add the columns for each arrow type separately and divide this number by the number of times you shot. If the average group size for the broadheads is more than one inch larger than the group size for the field points, you may have an accuracy problem with your broadheads. If you have any doubts, run the test again.

BROADHEADS
AND FIELD POINTS

A misconception many bowhunters have is that broadheads (hunting arrows) and field points (practice arrows) will always group together just because they weigh the same. Equipping arrows with the same weight heads will ensure the same spine and total arrow

weight, but not the same point of impact. The point of impact is where an arrow strikes a target in relation to where it was aimed. If you shoot more than one type of arrow (broadheads and field points) and they group in different locations, you can only adjust your shooting precisely for one or the other.

An arrow mounted with a broadhead literally has a guidance system on both ends of the arrow shaft—the blades and the fletching. The blades of the broadhead compete with the fletching for control of the arrow. Considering these facts, do not expect broadheads and field points always to have the same point of impact. All the bow tuning in the world will not guarantee that your practice and hunting arrows will group together. It will, however, move them as close together as possible. The most you can do is make sure you have perfect arrow flight and that your broadheads do not windplane.

The difference, if any, in the point of impact between your field points and broadheads depends on many variables. The more accurately you shoot, the simpler that difference will be for you to find. As a bowhunter, it is your responsibility to check the point of impact of your broadheads.

The sight shooter can correct point of impact problems by making the necessary adjustments to the sight. If you are an instinctive shooter, it is a little more complicated. As you practice, your mind and body work together and, over time, form an internal sight. If all of a sudden you shoot an arrow with a different point of impact, it is as if someone moved your sight and did not tell you.

To avoid this problem, instinctive shooters should consider the following suggestions.

1. Do everything possible to make sure your practice arrows and hunting arrows have the same point of impact.

2. Practice with only your hunting arrows prior to season.

If you have any doubts about your arrows having different points of impact, one solution is to have a very good sight shooter shoot both your practice and hunting arrows. This suggestion may offend some instinctive shooters, but it is the simplest and surest way to answer this important question. If you use this method for comparing your arrows, make sure your arrows are sufficient in length and that the spine is correct for the sight shooter's bow. First, have the sight shooter shoot both types of arrows from your maximum effective range. Next, measure the distance, if any, between the point of impact of the hunting and practice arrows. If this distance is over a few inches, you should practice only with your hunting arrows just before season or try to find a broadhead that has the same point of impact as your practice arrows.

Regardless of the point of impact issue, you should not sight-in or practice all summer long with field points, then just grab your broadheads and go hunting. Even if your broadheads and field points shoot in the same place, it is a good idea to practice with your broadheads often. You will automatically treat the arrow with more respect and think more about safety. It will also help with little subtleties, such as seeing something different on the end of your arrow shaft. Many bowhunters make a serious mistake by not practicing with broadhead-equipped arrows. You should keep several practice broadheads in good shooting condition at all times and use them as often as possible. Except for sharpness, I keep my hunting and practice broadheads in the same condition.

The larger the broadhead, the more potential for flight control problems. Here are a few suggestions to help remedy arrow flight problems when shooting broadhead-equipped arrows.

1. Make sure your bow is in proper tune.
2. Change broadheads. Try a smaller size, a different design or a lighter weight head.
3. Add more fletching; try helical fletch; try feathers.
4. Try an arrow with a stiffer spine.
5. Check for fletch contact with the arrow rest.

BROADHEAD ALIGNMENT

First, a short message about safety. I know this subject makes for boring reading but don't take razor-sharp broadheads lightly. If you do, one will get you sooner or later. When I was about 16, a fellow in our hunting party lost control of an arrow as he was putting on the string for a shot. He instinctively grabbed for the shaft as it fell to the ground. The arrow hit the ground, nock first, and the momentum from him reaching down, forced the broadhead through his hand. He not only lived but managed to hunt the next weekend. It seems both he and I were much tougher in those days and our broadheads duller than they should have been. Well, enough on safety; just remember always to be cautious when working with broadheads. You'll not see many deer from the doctor's office window.

Now, like the nock, all arrowheads—particularly broadheads—should be perfectly aligned with the arrow shaft. Fortunately, a broadhead that is out of alignment is fairly simple to recognize. The simplest way to find a misaligned broadhead is to do what is called a spin test (figure 46). To do this, find a hard, flat surface, such as an old table. Hold the arrow vertically, with the broadhead point on the table, then spin it like you would a top. If you

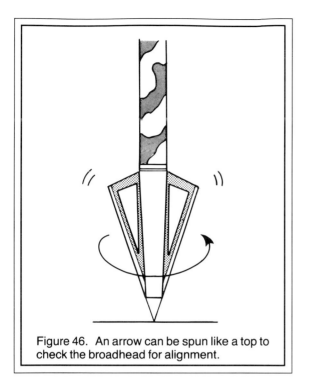

Figure 46. An arrow can be spun like a top to check the broadhead for alignment.

misaligned broadhead. But if you don't have an arrow straightener, a very inexpensive device can be made with four nails and a 2x4 or similar block of wood. Place the nails in the wood in an X shape about 15 inches apart. Place the arrow on the nails, look down on the broadhead from directly above and rotate the arrow (figure 47). For a point of reference, place a small round pencil mark directly below the tip of the broadhead. If the tip moves away and then back to this point as you rotate the arrow with your fingers, the broadhead is out of alignment. With some practice, you can learn to push the tip of the broadhead in the direction it needs to be moved. See figure 48 on the next page. Again this method will work on most heads.

A word of caution: when the point of a broadhead has been resharpened, it can be moved off center slightly. The traditional style heads are particularly susceptible to this prob-

can see more than a very slight wobble where the broadhead meets the shaft, accuracy and arrow flight could be adversely affected.

For problem arrows there are two cures. The first and easiest solution is simply to try a different head and then test again. This can be time consuming and I usually have a few problem arrows left over. For this reason, I use hot melt (Ferr-l-tite) to put in my inserts. By applying just the right amount of heat to the shaft, the insert will move but not fall out. For safety's sake, make sure to use pliers or a broadhead wrench for moving the head. Keeping the broadhead pointed up, move the head and insert inside the shaft with the pliers, let cool just a little, and spin test again. At some point in the 360-degree circle, the head will usually be significantly straighter. If I still have a problem arrow, I equip it with a field point and use it for practice.

Arrow straighteners can be used to spot a

Figure 47. A simple board and nails can be constructed to check broadheads and nocks for alignment.

Figure 48. After you spot which direction to push on the broadhead, a little pressure may help get it realigned.

lem. If this happens, the arrow may not spin properly but it should not affect arrow flight. If there appears to be an alignment problem, check to see if the point is lined up exactly with the center of the broadhead's ferrule. In other words, the point of the broadhead should be aligned with the center of the arrow shaft when the broadhead is installed.

SHOT PLACEMENT
AND THE BROADHEAD

Trying to find a bowhunter without an opinion on broadheads is like trying to find a huge whitetail buck at "high noon" on the last day of rifle season. I have observed over 200 big game animals harvested with archery equipment. Like many others, I have formed opinions about broadheads and shot placement. For many years, I have checked internally on harvested animals to learn how broadheads

perform and to see exactly what organs were struck. I also have kept records of the distance each animal traveled after the shot and the type of blood trail left by the animal. Despite field experiences, I always try to keep a non-prejudiced attitude toward broadhead design.

Over the years, my observations show that if a perfect shot is made, the contribution made by the sharpness of the broadhead is minimized. If, however, the shot is anything other than absolutely perfect, a razor-sharp broadhead's importance is paramount. The bigger than life fact is that animals can move in a heartbeat, jump the string or react in any number of unexpected ways. The best bowhunter in the world does not have complete control over shot placement. On the other hand, all of us have complete control over the sharpness of our broadheads and **there is never an acceptable reason for shooting anything less than a razor-sharp broadhead at a big game animal**.

Shot placement, not the broadhead you use, is the single most important factor in the humane harvest and recovery of big game animals. Although there is no question as to the importance of sharp broadheads and to a lesser degree broadhead size and design, putting it in the right place is the key. Here are two unusual examples of solid, double-lung shots to illustrate my feelings concerning shot placement and broadheads.

The first incident occurred on a Colorado elk hunt. An acquaintance of mine shot a bull elk with one of the first manufactured, replaceable blade heads. A broadside shot resulted in the arrow striking the elk through both lungs. I assisted with the tracking and field dressing of the bull. While skinning the elk, we found all three blades between the hide and the ribs on the entry side of the wound. The blades had been stripped from the broadhead before it reached the chest cavity. During most of the arrow travel within the elk, the broadhead was without blades. This literally amounted to shooting the elk with a target point; however, it traveled only 150 yards before collapsing. Obviously, the arrow placement through both lungs was far more important than any other factor in this particular situation.

Another incident occurred on a Wyoming antelope hunt where a friend shot at a buck and missed. Later, he mistakenly took the same used arrow from his quiver and shot a Pope and Young buck through both lungs. This antelope traveled less than 150 yards.

This certainly does not mean we should use dull or inferior broadheads. But again, these and many other experiences have indicated to me that shot placement is by far the single most important factor regarding animal recovery.

BROADHEAD SELECTION

The accuracy of each shot involves a multitude of factors, but those that relate directly to the broadhead are:

1. Flight characteristics, such as grouping capability, windplane and noise in flight.
2. Correct alignment of the broadhead with the shaft.
3. Broadhead weight, which can affect an arrow's balance, the spine of the shaft (stiffness) and the trajectory path of the arrow.

There are several important points to keep in mind when choosing a broadhead. Some broadheads, as mentioned, are more difficult to sharpen than others. You should know your capabilities in this area and make this a consideration. Below, listed by order of importance, are the considerations I use when selecting a broadhead. Sharpness is not included in this list only because **all broadheads must be razor-sharp before being used for hunting**.

1. Flight characteristics (accuracy).
2. Durability.
3. Weight.
4. Penetration.
5. Price.

Nothing is more important regarding penetration and harvesting game than an accurate, clean-flying arrow. Because of my strong belief that shot placement and the humane harvesting of big game animals are closely related, I have placed accuracy of the broadhead at the top of my list. Depending on your equipment, personal preferences, and type of big game you hunt, your list may vary.

Some may not agree with the location of penetration on my list but please permit me to explain. Because I shoot a heavy bow, my arrow starts out with 58 foot pounds of kinetic energy. Assuming there is good arrow flight, this will provide more than adequate penetration for all North American big game animals. I have harvested many elk, and these experiences have taught me that my equipment is not lacking in penetration. Penetration is important, but considering my equipment, the other concerns are even more important.

To determine the penetrating potential of your arrow, check the kinetic energy table at the end of this chapter. If your bow and arrow combination delivers less than 45 foot pounds of kinetic energy, you may want to consider the penetration benefits of a traditional style broadhead.

If you are uncertain about what broadhead to choose, I would suggest the following:

1. A cutting width of 1 to 1¼ inches.
2. A weight of 140 grains or less.

3. Three or four blades.
4. As for brand, choose from one of the many well established companies.

It has been said before but it is worthwhile saying again: Shoot the broadhead you like as long as it is razor sharp, strong and does not affect your arrow flight or accuracy.

As a consumer, I wish we had the selection of quality products available in all facets of the archery industry that we have in the broadhead segment. Quality products are available in the other areas, but have you noticed the selection of broadheads lately? Most of today's broadheads are of excellent quality. The one area with a limited selection of broadheads is in the lightweight division. Comparatively speaking, a few broadheads are manufactured that weigh less than 125 grains. Anderson Designs, Inc. (P.O. Box 605, Gladstone, NJ 07934) offers the largest selection of quality broadheads in this weight range (Figure 49), but they are expensive. Bowhunters are becoming increasingly aware of the advantages of a lightweight, fast moving arrow.

The broadhead is a significant amount of the

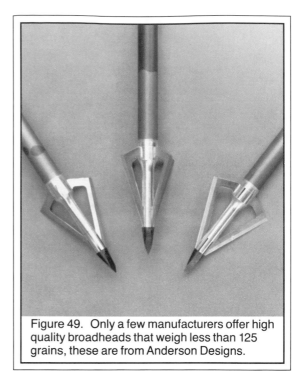

Figure 49. Only a few manufacturers offer high quality broadheads that weigh less than 125 grains, these are from Anderson Designs.

arrow's overall weight. Perhaps the selection of lightweight broadheads will increase with demand.

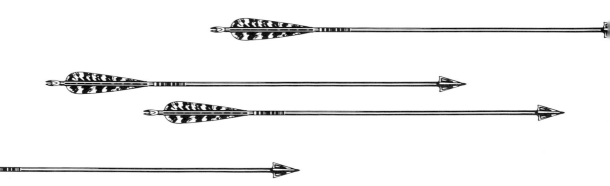

Kinetic Energy Table

					ARROW WEIGHT								
	400	425	450	475	500	525	550	575	600	625	650	675	700
170	25.7	27.3	28.9	30.5	32.1	33.7	35.3	36.9	38.5	40.1	41.7	43.3	44.9
175	27.2	28.9	30.6	32.3	34.0	35.7	37.4	39.1	40.8	42.5	44.2	45.9	47.6
180	28.8	30.6	32.4	34.2	36.0	37.8	39.6	41.4	43.2	45.0	46.8	48.6	50.4
185	30.4	32.3	34.2	36.1	38.0	39.9	41.8	43.7	45.6	47.5	49.4	51.3	53.2
190	32.1	34.1	36.1	38.1	40.1	42.1	44.1	46.1	48.1	50.1	52.1	54.1	56.1
195	33.8	35.9	38.0	40.1	42.2	44.3	46.5	48.6	50.7	52.8	54.9	57.0	59.1
200	35.5	37.8	40.0	42.2	44.4	46.6	48.9	51.1	53.3	55.5	57.7	60.0	62.2
205	37.3	39.7	42.0	44.3	46.7	49.0	51.3	53.7	56.0	58.3	60.7	63.0	65.3
210	39.2	41.6	44.1	46.5	49.0	51.4	53.9	56.3	58.8	61.2	63.7	66.1	68.6
215	41.1	43.6	46.2	48.8	51.3	53.9	56.5	59.0	61.6	64.1	66.7	69.3	71.9
220	43.0	45.7	48.4	51.1	53.7	56.4	59.1	61.8	64.5	67.2	69.9	72.6	75.2
225	45.0	47.8	50.6	53.4	56.2	59.0	61.8	64.7	67.5	70.3	73.1	75.9	78.7
230	47.0	49.9	52.9	55.8	58.7	61.7	64.6	67.6	70.5	73.4	76.4	79.3	82.2
235	49.1	52.1	55.2	58.3	61.3	64.4	67.5	70.5	73.6	76.7	79.7	82.8	85.9
240	51.2	54.4	57.6	60.8	64.0	67.2	70.4	73.6	76.8	80.0	83.1	86.4	89.6
245	53.3	56.7	60.0	63.3	66.7	70.0	73.3	76.7	80.0	83.3	86.7	90.0	93.3
250	55.5	59.0	62.5	66.0	69.4	72.9	76.3	79.8	83.3	86.8	90.2	93.7	97.2
255	57.8	61.4	65.0	68.6	72.2	75.8	79.4	83.0	86.7	90.3	93.9	97.5	101.1
260	60.1	63.8	67.6	71.3	75.1	78.8	82.6	86.3	90.1	93.8	97.6	101.3	105.1
265	62.4	66.3	70.2	74.1	78.0	81.9	85.8	89.7	93.6	97.5	101.4	105.3	109.2
270	64.8	68.8	72.9	76.9	81.0	85.0	89.1	93.1	97.1	101.2	105.2	109.3	113.3

ARROW SPEED

ACCESSORIES 10

This final chapter covers several bowhunting accessories and a few thoughts on pro shops. The items discussed are: The bow sight, mechanical release aids, a custom arrow rest that you can build, the bow quiver, the tackle box and its accessories. These items are optional, but some may offer a significant contribution to your bowhunting ability and enjoyment.

THE BOW SIGHT

It is a fair statement to say that a bow sight will help improve the shooting accuracy of the majority of bowhunters. This statement is true, however, only for bowhunters who have the basic fundamentals of shooting form under control.

When I was a youngster there were archery clubs that did not allow the use of bow sights. There are still clubs, particularly in the Midwest, where peer pressure is applied to discourage the use of bow sights. I must admit to disliking this type of attitude. Not everyone should use

a bow sight, but I am in favor of free choice and using what works best for you.

Here are two important objectives all bowhunters should strive for:

1. Do everything possible to prevent wounding an animal.
2. Enjoy bowhunting to the fullest.

Because of the added accuracy, a bow sight helps me to prevent wounding animals and, consequently, enhances my enjoyment of the sport. As with all optional equipment, it is best to understand what a bow sight has to offer. Then make your own decision whether or not you would like to use one.

As mentioned, a bow sight helps most bowhunters shoot more accurately. To function properly, it must be sighted-in and locked in place. The danger with a bow sight is that it can loosen during shooting or become bent. If either of these situations occurs and goes undetected, it could be trouble city. Once sighted-in, the sight should be marked with a scribe for an easy reference point. As a precaution, this mark should be checked for alignment and the screws checked for tightness on a regular basis.

CHOOSING A BOW SIGHT

A bow sight (figure 50) should offer the following features:

1. RUGGED CONSTRUCTION—There is actually a sight on the market that, in my opinion, is overbuilt. I did not think I would ever say that because I like my equipment to be tough. The only problem with this sight is the weight. Many times, I carry my bow all day long, and weight is a concern. A sight should be strong without being overly heavy.

2. PIN GUARD—A pin guard should be reasonably stout. When checking bows with arrow flight problems, it is not unusual to find the pin guard set too low. This will cause the fletching of the arrow to strike the pin guard when the arrow is released. To check this situation, place lipstick on the pin guard and shoot a few arrows. Next, check the pin guard for smudges in the lipstick. Also, check the arrows for telltale signs of lipstick on the fletching. If you find any sign of contact, move the pin guard up and retest.

3. ADJUSTABILITY—The sight should provide for easy and adequate adjustments. Most of today's sights have two pin slots. This provides more room between the pins, allowing more convenient adjustment of today's faster bows.

The sight should also provide for an up and down adjustment of the entire sight. This is necessary because of the variable factors such as riser design, individual shooting style and anchor points. Other items, such as cross hairs or pins, are a matter of personal taste.

SIGHTING-IN

Once the sight is properly attached, the next step is to sight-in your bow. An easy way to remember which direction to move the sight pins is that you **always move the sight pin in the direction that the arrow strikes**. If the shot is high, you move the sight pin up; if the shot is to the right, you move the sight pin to the right, etc.

A bow should be sighted-in for exact yardages (see chapter on "Range Estimation"). Make sure you always personally verify the yardages at the location you choose to sight-in your bow. From this point, I prefer to sight-in to even 10-yard distances, starting with 20 yards. Allow me to explain why.

There are two reasons I start with a 20-yard sight setting. First, I get few shot opportunities under 20 yards. Second, trajectory is not that severe inside 20 yards. Attempting a 10-yard

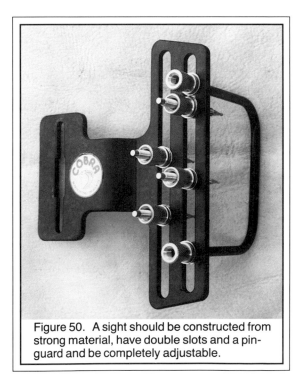

Figure 50. A sight should be constructed from strong material, have double slots and a pin-guard and be completely adjustable.

shot using the 20-yard pin will require that you hold only a few inches below the desired point of impact. It would not be necessary to hold off the body when attempting a shot at a big game animal under these conditions. If you use both a 10- and 20-yard pin, you are almost duplicating a sight setting unless you are using lightweight equipment. One exception to starting with 20 yards would be if you expect very close-range shots from treestands.

If your first pin is set for 20 yards, it is a good idea to practice from 10 to 20 yards. You may be surprised how little "hold under" is required to hit a target at 10 yards aiming with your 20-yard pin.

After the 20-yard pin is sighted-in, I set the rest of my pins for even 10-yard increments—30, 40, etc. With the sight pins set at every 10 yards, I use them in the following manner. Using the distance between 25 and 34 yards as an example:

I place an animal estimated to be 25 yards away, exactly between the 20- and 30-yard pins, using both pins for windage (figure 51 A). If I believe the animal to be 27 to 28 yards away, I hold the 30-yard pin just below the bottom of the animal's chest (figure 51 B). For an animal I estimate to be at 29 to 31 yards, I hold the 30-yard pin exactly where I want to hit (figure 51 C). For a 32- to 33-yard shot, I hold the 30-yard pin at the top of the animal's back (figure 51 D). This method works best on big game animals because of their size.

If the above format sounds complicated, in the reality of a hunting situation, it is simplified considerably. Again, using the distances between 25 and 34 as an example:

At the time of the shot, I simply make one of the following choices: 25, short 30, 30 dead on, or long 30. By using this method, I am forced to consider the exact yardage and make my very best estimate. With this system, I am

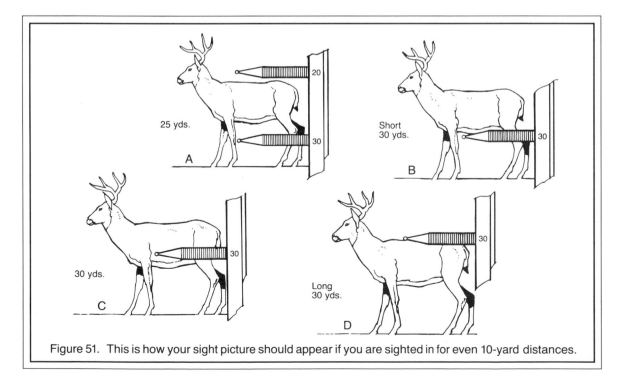

Figure 51. This is how your sight picture should appear if you are sighted in for even 10-yard distances.

never required to "hold off" the animal very far.

When estimating the distance to an animal, make sure you do not get in the habit of shooting for even yardages only. The law of averages won't put more than one in 10 animals at even 10-yard distances.

An interesting phenomenon that usually occurs at very close range is that you may need to aim with your 20-yard pin to hit a small object at 5 yards. This method of sighting is only necessary starting at about 6 to 8 yards. At these distances, and under, you must use a pin sighted-in for a greater distance, possibly the 20- or even 30-yard pin. In other words, at extremely close range, the aiming process is reversed; the closer the target, the lower the sight pin must be set to hit that target. The exact distance that this change takes place varies from shooter to shooter because of facial structure and the anchor point location. The lower the anchor point, the more acute the situation becomes.

The only time I use this sighting method is when attempting to shoot rattlesnakes, carp or frogs at very close range. This is something you will not use very often, although it is interesting to see how it works.

The sight I use is designed to facilitate a quick change of the pin portion of the sight. This is an excellent feature in that it permits the shooter to quickly match the sight bar to the type of arrows he wishes to shoot. This requires carrying extra sight bars with you and sighting them in ahead of time for each type of arrow you intend to shoot—broadheads, field points, wood blunts, etc. Once this has been accomplished, the sight bars can be exchanged in less than a minute.

In good faith, I cannot recommend the brand of bow sight I use because of the poor quality of its construction. This sight is made from lightweight, soft metal and it bends far too

readily for rugged use. I am extremely cautious with my bow, but I have found my sight bent on several occasions without knowing how it happened.

To me, this is a strong example of a manufacturer's taking an excellent idea and still producing a borderline product. This company has been good about replacing the bent sights but there comes a time when the trouble is more hassle than it is worth. We, as bowhunters, must scrutinize each intended purchase and speak up when equipment does not function adequately.

MECHANICAL RELEASE AIDS

You might be surprised at the number of bowhunters who consider a mechanical release an important part of their hunting equipment. Some bowhunters, however, are adamantly opposed to anyone using a mechanical release. They have a right to their opinion, but it is just as much your right to use a release if you choose. If you do choose to use a mechanical release, make sure it is legal in each state in which you plan to hunt. Releases are legal in most states but, it is always best to check to make sure you are not violating the law.

My experience with releases has shown me that they give many bowhunters both an extra measure of control over buck fever and improved accuracy, which, in turn, reduces their chances of wounding an animal. For that I am thankful. But releases are certainly not for everyone.

A release is more difficult to use than fingers for timed or hurried shots because it should be squeezed slowly to maintain consistent accuracy. Squeezing a release slowly is the key to ensuring that the shooter does not anticipate the shot and flinch. This is the reason releases do not adapt well to rushed shots. In some cases, when using a release, you will not be able to get the shot off when it would have been quite possible for a finger shooter.

If you are inclined to try a release, it will take plenty of getting used to, so give it some time. Chances are you will be pleased with the results. If possible, ask the assistance of a shooter who is familiar with shooting a release.

It is best not to purchase a release without trying it first. Your best bet should be the local pro shop, but don't give up if you can't find a release that suits you. There are many releases on the market and most pro shops carry only a limited selection. If you do not find something you like, check mail order catalogs, archery magazines and other pro shops. Quality releases are expensive, so don't make a mistake in your choice. There are two basic styles of releases that work well for the bowhunter: the concho style (figure 52 A) and the three-finger, or T-, style (figure 52 B). The main difference

between the two styles is the position of the hand while holding the release. It is likely that there are 20 or more different models available in each style, but the first problem is to choose the style of release that is the most comfortable and accurate for you.

Holding a concho style release places your shooting hand in a position similar to that depicted in figure 53, and most models are triggered by the index finger. Because of this hand position, it is difficult for most shooters to locate a solid anchor point. For this reason, the majority of shooters using a concho style release will also require a peep sight to reach their full potential in shooting accuracy. For a further explanation of the peep sight, see the chapter on "The Bow and String."

Most three-finger style releases place your shooting hand in a position similar to that depicted in figure 54 on the next page. They are often triggered by the thumb or little finger.

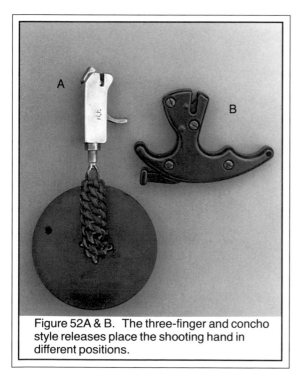

Figure 52A & B. The three-finger and concho style releases place the shooting hand in different positions.

Figure 53. The concho style release places the hand in this position when at anchor.

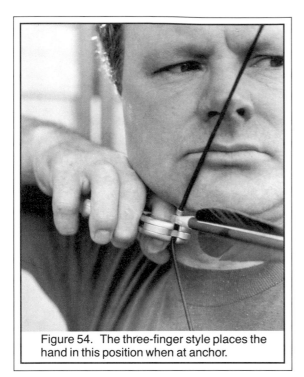

Figure 54. The three-finger style places the hand in this position when at anchor.

1. With rope, which then attaches to some type of triggering device (figure 55 A).
2. With mechanical "fingers" that close directly on the string (figure 55 B).

THE ROPE RELEASE

The rope style release accomplishes two important tasks. First, the rope gives or twists, which minimizes any existing torque and makes it less important to keep the shooting hand level. Second, the rope, being soft, causes very little damage to the bowstring serving. Rope style releases are used by many serious tournament shooters for these reasons.

An inconvenient characteristic of the rope style releases is that they can be slow and cumbersome to use in a hunting situation. They can be difficult to attach to the bowstring. Nevertheless, a person who shoots in competition or who uses a rope release frequently during practice can certainly make one work

Holding a three-finger style release causes a gap to form between the index and second finger. Most archers then align the jaw bone in the gap between these two fingers for their anchor point. Some shooters are fortunate to find that a peep sight is not necessary when using a three-finger style release. A peep sight will, however, always improve a shooter's accuracy, though in varying degrees. On the negative side, a peep sight is difficult for many bowhunters to use under some hunting conditions, such as low-light and hurried or timed shots.

My advice is to use the release for some time, get used to it, and see how your accuracy comes along. If you are not happy, add a peep later. Unfortunately, no one can make these choices for you; however, it is helpful to get advice from your local pro shop.

Regardless of style, releases attach to the bowstring in one of two distinct ways:

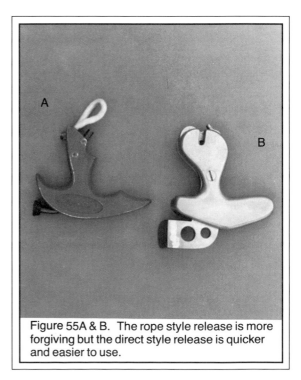

Figure 55A & B. The rope style release is more forgiving but the direct style release is quicker and easier to use.

for hunting. It just takes more time to become proficient at preparing for a shot quickly with a rope release.

THE DIRECT RELEASE TYPE

It is easier to become accustomed to attaching a direct type release to the bowstring. A direct style release should offer the following qualities. The most important of these, second only to quality construction, is the quiet self-loading and unloading feature. This means you should be able to attach the release to the string silently by pushing the release gently onto the bowstring. This is accomplished by depressing the trigger as you move the release onto the string. Then, releasing the trigger should silently lock it into place. The silent aspect is extremely important in close hunting situations but not all manufacturers incorporate this feature into their releases.

A rotating head is important to shooters who have a tendency to torque or twist the string when they are at full draw. The rotating head gives to any pressure, which allows the shooter to place his hand in any comfortable anchor position without exerting torque on the string. In this way, it is similar to a rope release. Not all shooters need this feature. It depends on the normal position of the shooting hand when it is locked at your anchor point.

When using a direct style release, some shooters attach an additional nock locator (the same type as used for the nocking point) just below the arrow when it is on the string (figure 56). This prevents direct contact between the nock of the arrow and the release. The extra nock locator is not necessary when using a rope style release. Some release manufacturers also recommend the additional nock locator, believing that it will improve accuracy. If an additional nock locator is recommended, this information should be included with the release.

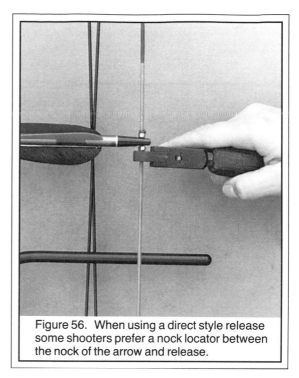

Figure 56. When using a direct style release some shooters prefer a nock locator between the nock of the arrow and release.

A multitude of releases are available. Try to select a model that allows you to have a solid and comfortable anchor point. Tru-Fire Corporation, (732 State St., North Fond Du Lac, WI 54935) offers a good selection of releases. When purchasing a release, remember that any noise made by the release in the archery shop will sound ten times louder in a real hunting situation.

One manufacturer recently brought out a release whose name supposedly indicated its high quality. This particular release sounded like a firing squad locking and loading as it was attached to the string. In some respects, it is indeed an excellent release, but I would not want it within five miles of my bear or whitetail stand.

THE ARROW REST

The purpose of the arrow rest is to hold the

arrow on the bow in exactly the same position until the bowstring is released. It should then cause as little interference with the shaft and fletching as possible. Bowhunters generally need a stronger, more silent arrow rest than their target-shooting counterparts. For these reasons, care should be exercised in your selection of an arrow rest. There are many adequate hunting arrow rests on the market today. Some good rests are offered by Golden Key (P.O. Box 1446, Montrose, CO 81401).

The perfect arrow rest should accomplish the following:

1. Support the arrow with good strength from below and give reasonable support from both sides. The arrow should stay on the rest even if you lightly bump or jolt the bow. The arrow should also stay on the rest when you have the arrow nocked and the bow hanging near your treestand, even with the wind blowing.
2. Permit the arrow to be shot without the arrow fletching contacting the rest. This is particularly important when shooting vanes.
3. Permit the shooter to draw the arrow silently.
4. Be rugged, long lasting and easy to adjust.

Devices are available to help hold the arrow on the rest. Personally, I prefer not to use additional equipment when it can be avoided. I am able to do without the additional arrow-holding device because my arrow rest supports the arrow securely enough to meet my needs.

For many years the selection of arrow rests was poor. After a long period of trial and error, I developed my own arrow rest system.

As mentioned before, there are many good arrow rests available today, but I prefer my design over anything currently on the market.

This arrow rest is not on the market, but you can make it yourself. The rest is not difficult to construct; however, you must get the parts from three separate sources. Figure 57 shows the arrow rest parts and the completed arrow rest. Figure 58 shows the arrow rest as it appears on a bow from different angles. On the following page are the detailed instructions on how to build the rest.

First, it is best to purchase a Pacesetter II Arrow Rest made by Golden Key Futura and offered by most archery dealers. This rest includes the necessary cushion plunger to be used with the rest you are about to make. Next, you will need some Bear mohair from Bear Archery. Make sure you use the real Bear mohair and not the less expensive material because this is what makes the rest so good. The last item you will need is a section of feeler gauge material. This material works the best in .0015 or .0016 thickness, which can be purchased in one-foot lengths at precision tool

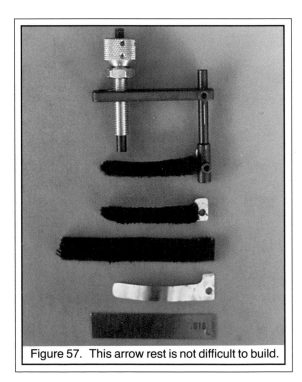

Figure 57. This arrow rest is not difficult to build.

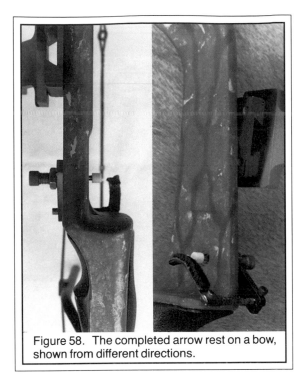

Figure 58. The completed arrow rest on a bow, shown from different directions.

shops.

You will also need a good pair of aviation shears, a sharp, ⅛-inch drill bit, an electric grinder and a high-quality solvent.

1. Cut the feeler gauge material into 3-inch lengths.
2. Center punch and drill the ⅛-inch hole ¼-inch from either end.
3. Shape the feeler gauge stock on a grinder, keeping some water handy while grinding. Do not allow the feeler gauge material to overheat because it will become brittle and severely shorten the life of the rest. I have found the rest works best ¼- to ⅜-inch wide. Once the basic shaping is completed, place the rest in the arm provided with the Pacesetter II rest and grind off the sharp corners.
4. Now, with your fingers, shape the feeler gauge material in a gentle arch, making the highest point exactly at the cushion plunger. All this shaping can be accomplished by hand. Then cut the material to length about ½- to ¾-inch beyond the cushion plunger and round off the sharp corners on the grinder. Place a very slight twist in the feeler gauge material to the cushion plunger side. Be careful; very little is needed. In fact, the rest will work fine without the twist after an arrow track develops in the mohair.
5. Cut the mohair slightly larger than the feeler gauge material. Now clean the feeler gauge material with the high-quality solvent and attach the mohair. The mohair comes with a self-adhesive back that works well most of the time. If you prefer something more permanent, use 3M gasket cement. Trim the excess mohair with a razor blade.
6. When adjusting the rest, make sure the arrow rides in the center of the cushion plunger for the up and down adjustment. For the right and left adjustment, leave at least a ⅛- to ¼-inch gap between the end of the cushion plunger and the near edge of the rest.
7. The new rest will soon form an arrow track or groove in the mohair, making it very stable.
8. To check for fletch clearance through this, or any, arrow rest, put some bright colored lipstick on the fletch of one arrow. Shoot the marked arrow and immediately check the rest for telltale signs of fletch contact.
9. Drawing the arrow across the cushion plunger may emit a noise. To help eliminate this noise, wax the arrow shaft and the tip of the cushion plunger with a good grade of auto wax.

Vane-fletched arrows can be used with this type of rest. But like most arrow rests, it must be set up to avoid contact with the vanes. Use the lipstick test mentioned above and refer to *Tuning Your Compound Bow* by Larry Wise for more information on improving arrow flight in general.

THE TACKLE BOX AND BOW CASE

When you travel by air, a plastic or metal box becomes necessary to protect your bow. When traveling by vehicle, I have found a soft, well-padded, zipper-type bow case and a converted fishing tackle box (figure 59) for accessories are most convenient.

Many bowhunters try to carry everything they could possibly need with them while hunting, instead of having a well-supplied tackle box as close as possible. Regardless of the method you use to carry your extra equipment, there are several items you should have avail-

Figure 59. A fishing tackle box is a handy way to carry small accessories.

able at all times for maintenance and repair. For example, when I am hunting from a base camp on a daily basis, I take nothing more than an extra bow string for repairs. On a backpack trip, I take minimal equipment for repairs; but again, I do have my tackle box in the nearest base camp or vehicle.

The first list below includes necessary items; the second lists optional items. You can eliminate the obvious items from both lists if your equipment does not require them. An example would be a one-piece recurve bow with a quiver that does not require an allen wrench.

1. Two extra bowstrings ready to use; one can be taped to the arm between the top and bottom of the bow quiver.
2. Bowstring wax.
3. Allen wrench set.
4. Extra arrow rest.
5. Fletching cement.
6. Dental floss.
7. Nock locator.
8. Nock set pliers.
9. Broadhead and knife sharpening device.
10. Extra broadheads and/or replacement blades.
11. Bow square for checking nocking point and bow tiller.
12. Small pliers.
13. Broadhead wrench.
14. Extra armguard.
15. Extra glove, tab or release.

OPTIONAL EQUIPMENT:

1. Nocks.
2. Inserts.
3. Ferr-L-Tite broadhead and insert glue.
4. Large butane lighter or candle for changing inserts or broadheads (arrow repair).
5. Extra sight pins and parts.
6. Small file.
7. Extra cushion plunger.

8. Bow Dull (camo paint).
9. Tape.
10. Lubrication (oil).
11. Locktite.
12. Extra compass.
13. Extra small flashlight.
14. Extra silencers.
15. Scent.
16. String server.
17. Measuring device (100-ft. tape or marked rope).
18. Camo face paint.
19. Screw driver.
20. Extra knife.
21. Razor blades.
22. Super glue.
23. Scissors.
24. Rubber bands; can double as silencers.

Another helpful addition to the tackle box is goose or duck down. The reason I did not include down in the above list is that it takes some explaining.

Down is the best wind detector around because it allows you to see the changing wind currents. I carry down in addition to the wind detector on my bow while hunting on foot. But down is most beneficial when you are placing or hunting from treestands. Down can show you the changing wind currents or the exact location from which an approaching buck is going to detect your scent. Once, while hunting elk from a treestand, I released some down into a light breeze only to have it pass by 40 yards away going in the opposite direction over a minute later.

Down is relatively easy to come by inexpensively or free. Here are some ideas:

1. Down clothing manufacturers clean up every working day. They have saved down for me on several occasions.
2. Check old down coats, pillows, and sleeping bags.
3. If you or your friends hunt waterfowl, save the down as the birds are plucked.

Down can be messy to carry, but a little goes a long way. I carry my down in ziplock plastic bags with some needle holes to let the air out.

What you carry in your tackle box will, in all likelihood, vary considerably from my list. But it is far better to carry a little extra tackle than to be short that critical item in an emergency.

What extras you take along may depend on the length and destination of your hunting trip. Try to plan ahead. Don't allow a small item to cost you valuable hunting time.

G. Fred Asbell, President of the Pope and Young Club, related the following story. A bowhunter, who shall remain nameless, was so excited about his upcoming hunting trip that he arrived at the outfitter's camp several days early. Unfortunately, during the pre-dawn hustle and bustle of opening day, his bowstring was cut. Obviously, I would not be writing about this situation had he brought along a spare string. The end result was that it took two days to find a shop with the right length string and another half day to get it set up because he didn't know how. The unfortunate part of this story is that this bowhunter's reason for not having a spare string could not be lack of time to prepare (he arrived several days early). It could not be a money problem because he was on a very expensive guided hunt. The only reasons left are a lack of knowledge and just not planning ahead. Don't let something like this happen to you.

THE BOW QUIVER

The bow quiver is by far the most popular means of carrying broadheads while hunting. Today, it is rather rare to find a bowhunter who does not consider a bow quiver part of his equipment. Like almost everything, bow quivers have a few disadvantages, but I have found them to be the most convenient way to carry broadhead-equipped arrows.

The subject of safety and quivers has been addressed by many writers and, as a general rule, bowhunters are well educated in this regard. All broadheads must be completely covered to provide the proper measure of safety. If you come in contact with anyone carrying uncovered broadheads, you certainly have the right, if not an obligation, to speak up. Most of today's quivers provide an adequate margin of safety when used correctly.

When choosing what is known as a quick detachable (or QD) quiver, make sure you select a well-built model. Most QD quivers have one lockdown point which allows them to be removed quickly, but this is a potential weak spot if not designed properly (figure 60). Some QD quivers are well-designed. In fact, I

am using one at this time with satisfactory results. But the most stable bow quivers are generally two-piece and have separate attachments for the top and bottom sections.

If you choose a QD, or any other one-piece quiver, try to avoid all models with plastic frames. This does not include the hood, which is often made from plastic materials. Metal frame quivers are more expensive but they are quieter, more stable, longer-lasting, and in the long run a better value for your money.

Another point I consider important in a quiver is its adjustability. I prefer a quiver that will adjust to an angle that places the fletch end of most of my arrows between the lower limb and the bow string. This creates a more compact unit and helps prevent contact with brush during a stalk.

The material used to hold the broadhead inside the hood can be made of anything from light foam to a pliable rubber substance. If the quiver you are considering is equipped with a light spongy foam, you will be replacing it often, even if you are careful and align the broadheads in the same cuts each time. But placing the broadheads exactly in the same cuts will increase the life of the foam regardless of its quality and is a good practice to follow on all bow quivers.

Bow quivers come in various sizes from 4- to 16-arrow models. This is a very personal choice, but I prefer an 8-arrow model. I like to carry 3 blunts and 5 broadheads. I use the blunts for stump shooting, checking distances from blinds, hunting small game or just having fun. Over the years, there have been many occasions when I have broken or lost all my blunts but never all the broadheads. I find that blunts remain more stable in most bow quivers when the nock end is placed in the foam. In other words, the blunts are reversed from the broadheads. Another solution is to cut small holes in the foam the size of your blunts.

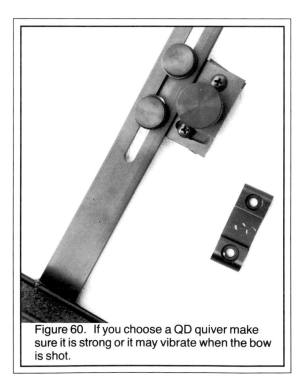

Figure 60. If you choose a QD quiver make sure it is strong or it may vibrate when the bow is shot.

Adding a quiver to your bow can change the point of impact of the arrows. The more accurately you shoot, the easier it will be to spot a point of impact change. It is, however, always best to sight-in and practice with your bow set up exactly like you plan to use it in the field. If you plan to remove your bow quiver when hunting from a stand, keep this point in mind and practice ahead of time.

In addition to bow quivers, there are back and hip broadhead quivers. These quivers are no longer very popular but offer bowhunters who prefer not to use a bow quiver some alternatives. For more information on these options, check with your local pro shop.

THE PRO SHOP

Several times throughout this book, I have recommended your local pro shop. Not wanting you to think I have a special interest in pro shops, allow me to explain my position.

There are excellent pro shops and terrible pro shops. Most are somewhere in between. Just because you go to a pro shop does not guarantee you will get the best advice or the truth about a product. On the other hand, you may get very competent assistance. But play it safe—do as much research as possible on your own, ask questions, compare products, get a second opinion.

Most pro shops charge retail price for their merchandise and, consequently, should provide the following:

1. A hands-on demonstration of the product you intend to purchase.
2. Competent advice.
3. Service.

If you are unhappy with the selection, advice or service you get from your local pro shop, speak up and ask to talk to the owner. Most pro shops are privately owned. If you like your local pro shop and enjoy having it nearby, give it your support. Without your support, it may not be there when you need it the most.

Mail order businesses are another option and they can save you money. But they are not available to give you advice. You must also choose each item from a picture and wait for it to be delivered. If you are sure about the item you want and are not in a rush, a reputable mail order house is a viable alternative.

EPILOGUE

Because of a serious injury that was unrelated to bowhunting, completing this book often seemed an impossible task. Each time I was ready to throw in the towel, friends stepped in with hard work and encouragement. If you enjoyed the book, they are the ones who deserve the lion's share of the credit.

I seriously doubt that anyone will ever get rich by writing a book about bowhunting, and I can honestly say that this book was not written with that intent. It was written to share knowledge about a sport I love. I truly hope I have accomplished that goal.

Knowledge seems to command little respect in today's society. Many search for the short cut—the easy way to success. Bowhunters as a group are no different. We want a broadhead that will leave a heavy bloodtrail even when the animal is hit in the hoof, as well as a scent that will work magic regardless of our other mistakes. The quick fix, in most cases, proves not to be a very satisfying or dependable solution.

On the other hand, a combination of knowledge, the proper attitude and hard work will never let you down. I believe you will find this particularly true with bowhunting. All veteran bowhunters have had many successful hunts without harvesting an animal.

If you enjoy bowhunting as much as I do, I hope we have the chance to meet. Should our paths cross, don't hesitate to say hello. If you feel this book has something to offer, please share it with another bowhunter.

Before closing, I would like to express a personal thought about our sport. Bowhunting should not be a contest among men. It should only be a contest between man and animal up to the time when we are successful at getting a good close-range shot. At that moment, the hunter has already succeeded and he or she should be proud of that success. As for making the shot, the only real competition comes from within.

If you hunt only to impress others, please reconsider your motives. The highest reward for the bowhunter is not the animal he harvests but rather what he becomes by the challenge of the hunt. Speaking in 1887, Sioux Chief Yellow Lark, in my opinion, summed up the essence of bowhunting with these words: "Make me strong, not to be superior to my brothers, but to fight my greatest enemy—myself...."

Good luck and good hunting!

Dave Holt
Denver, Colorado
June, 1988

READING LIST

INSTRUCTIONAL SHOOTING BOOKS:

Winning Archery, by Al Henderson. 1983
   Available from: Target Communications Corporation (7626 W. Donges Bay Rd. Mequon, WI 53092).

Archery for Beginners, by John Williams. 1985
   Available from: Contemporary Books (180 N. Michigan Ave. Chicago, IL 60601).

Instinctive Shooting, by G. Fred Asbell. 1988.
   Available from: Historical Times, Inc. (P.O. Box 8200, 2245 Kohn Rd. Harrisburg, PA 17105).

BOW-TUNING:

Tuning Your Compound Bow, by Larry Wise. 1985.
   Available from: Target Communications Corporation (7626 W. Donges Bay Rd. Mequon, WI 53092).

GENERAL BOWHUNTING INFORMATION:

Bowhunters Encyclopedia, by Dwight Schuh. 1987.
   Available from: Dwight Schuh (Rt. 1, P.O. Box 1322 A Nampa, ID 83651).

Successful Bowhunting, by M. R. James. 1985.
   Available from: Historical Times, Inc. (P.O. Box 8200, 2245 Kohn Rd. Harrisburg, PA 17105).

HOW-TO-HUNT BOOKS:

Bowhunting for Mule Deer, by Dwight Schuh. 1984-1985.
   Available from: Dwight Schuh (Rt. 1, P.O. Box 1322 A Nampa, ID 83651).

Bugling for Elk, by Dwight Schuh. 1983.
   Available from: Dwight Schuh (Rt. 1, P.O. Box 1322 A Nampa, ID 83651).

Black Bears, by Bob McGuire. 1983.
   Available from: Bowhunting Productions (P.O. Box 873 Blountville, TN 37617).

INDEX